WHO SAYS KIDS DON'T COME WITH A MANUAL?

Louanne Saenz, Ed.S., L.P.C.

PublishAmerica
Baltimore

© 2004 by Louanne Saenz.
All rights reserved. No part of this book may be reproduced, stored in a retrieval system or transmitted in any form or by any means without the prior written permission of the publishers, except by a reviewer who may quote brief passages in a review to be printed in a newspaper, magazine or journal.

First printing

ISBN: 1-4137-2761-1
PUBLISHED BY PUBLISHAMERICA, LLLP
www.publishamerica.com
Baltimore

Printed in the United States of America

Dedication

To my children, Diana, Alex, and Carl.
You not only exceeded my expectations, you fulfilled my dreams.
To my husband René,
If all children had a father like you, we wouldn't need counselors.

ACKNOWLEDGMENTS

Many people have had a hand in the development of this book. Thanks to my family who allowed me the chance to create my vision of family through them. Thanks to the families at Loon Lake Elementary. While I was hired to teach and counsel you, I have become all the wiser because of you. I want to recognize my own parents, for always pushing me to lengths I never thought I could reach. Many, many thanks to Kevin Reside, President of KAND Technology for recovering my book from my corrupt floppy disk! Finally I'd like to acknowledge my friend and neighbor, Dr. Dan Greenberg, whose frank input helped me crystallize my thoughts and views.

Table of Contents

Section 1: ANALYZING OUR BEHAVIORS   15
- A. Guilt   17
- B. Justice   19
- C. Values   21
- D. Who Owns the Problem?   24
- E. "Reduce not Eliminate",   28
      "Replace not Erase"   29
- F. You Can Make a Difference   31
- G. Zeroing In on the Issue   33

Section 2: BASIC HUMAN NEEDS   35
- A. Behavior   37
- B. Fun   45
- C. Independence   48
- D. Love   52
- E. Power   55

Section 3: COMMUNICATING WITH OUR CHILDREN   59
- A. Empathy   61
- B. Emotional Intelligence   63
- C. Humor   66
- D. Messages   68
- E. No!   71
- F. Praise vs. Encouragement   74
- G. Questioning   76
- H. Quiet   78
- I. Remorse   79
- J. Rehearse   81
- K. "Rewind the Video"   83
- L. Expectations   85
- M. Example   88
- N. "You Have to Try it. You Don't Have to Like it."   90
- O. Talking to Your Children (Summary)   91

Section 4: **DISCIPLINE** — 95
- A. Discipline — 97
- B. Consequences — 100
- C. Influence — 103
- D. Motivation — 106
- E. Rewards / Punishment — 111

Section 5: **HOME SURVIVAL** — 115
- A. Allowances — 117
- B. Allergies / Antibiotics — 119
- C. Bedtime — 121
- D. Chores — 123
- E. Kitchen Capers — 126

Section 6: **SCHOOL SURVIVAL** — 129
- A. Homework — 131
- B. Literacy — 136
- C. "What Can I Do at Home?" — 140
- D. Extracurricular Activities — 144

Section 7: **IMPROVING RELATIONSHIPS** — 145
- A. Attention — 147
- B. Friendships — 149
- C. Getting Revenge — 152
- D. Opportunities — 154
- E. Sibling Rivalry — 156
- F. Stress / Spirituality / Support — 159
- G. Undoing Our Mistakes — 162

INTRODUCTION

Raising my children has truly been a labor of love. That's not to say I didn't have those times when I was throwing their clothes out the window, or yelling so loud the neighbors could hear. Those moments do pale, though, compared to all the other wonderful times we've had.

As this book evolved in my mind, I knew I wanted to write something that was practical and easily read. Having both the personal and professional experience of dealing with children for almost thirty years, I have to say I learned things not taught in a classroom, doctor's or therapist's office. My intention is to address the most common concerns I have encountered between parents and children. Every recommendation or trial run in this manual, I have tested with my own children or have recommended to parents. Only the successes are presented to you in these pages.

I will be stressing three themes throughout this book:

1. **Change must start with the adults.**
   The only behavior we truly can control is our own. Before parents can ever begin to impact their children's behavior, they need to know and understand their own reactions to their children. When their reactions change, then their children will most likely adjust their behavior.

2. **Influence, influence, influence your children!**
   A parent always hopes their advice to their children is heeded. If adults get beyond the concept of rewards and punishment, their advice and influence becomes important. Begin by thinking of the people who have influenced you. Why do you respect them enough to heed their advice, and let them influence your behavior?

3.   Go easy on yourself.
As parents, we are always second-guessing our decisions. Just as with dieting, every day is a fresh start. Some days we can resist temptation, and other days we simply give in to our children or tempers. Knowing and admitting our mistakes is all part of the challenge.

It is with pleasure that I share what I have learned over the years. I hope your job as parents is made just a little easier by what you learn in this manual!

Section 1:

ANALYZING OUR BEHAVIORS:

    A. Guilt
    B   Justice
    C. Values
    D   Who Owns the Problem?
    E. "Reduce not Eliminate", "Replace not Erase"
    F. You Can Make a Difference
    G. Zeroing In on the Issue

GUILT

Guilt can be a destructive emotion, particularly when it comes to raising children. When my children were very young, I attended my first parenting class. I remember the facilitator talking about "guilt based" vs. "confidence based" parenting. It was one of the most powerful lessons I ever learned, and am glad to pass it on to you. Many situations will exist that force us to decide based upon the emotions of guilt or confidence. Obviously the more we parent with confidence, the easier it will be to stand firm to our decisions, and avoid opportunities for power struggles. However this is usually not the case with today's parents. We always have an excuse to feel guilty or second- guess our parenting skills. We think things like, "oh I work all day, so here's something extra to make up for missed time.", or "poor thing, I'm not home to do it for them." Newly-divorced parents are heavy on guilt, and give in when they know they shouldn't have. We live in a society that easily develops a "victim" mentality, rather than a "survivor" mentality. Feeling guilty or confident is a definite choice, however.

When I returned to work full-time after being home a few years, I remember feeling guilty about not being able to do as much for my children. My youngest was only in first grade, but I quickly erased that from my mind. Instead I thought, "This will be an opportunity for them to learn independence." We went shopping and picked out alarm clocks, came home and made schedules of their morning routines, and the adjustment went smoothly. Guilt sometimes returned, especially when they got sick, for example, but I was fortunate enough to have my parents nearby and they gladly watched them and my kids loved the attention. When you think about many of your parenting situations, that have the potential to cause guilt, try to rethink it before you begin doubting yourself.

Louanne Saenz

EXERCISE:
Think of situation that you currently feel GUILTY about:

EXAMPLE: *"I wish I could be there when they get home from school."*

_____
_____

Now restate it to a CONFIDENT statement.

Example: *"They like having Kim as a babysitter after school. I do get to be there all summer and their other vacations."*

_____
_____

NOTE: If you honestly can't switch it to a confident statement, then is it truly something you should be guilty about, and genuinely needs some adjustment? Before you start beating yourself up, though, make sure you get some other people's opinions about your situation.

JUSTICE

I want to briefly discuss justice because children's interpretation of that word is that everyone gets treated equally. The reality of it, however, is that "Fair is not always equal." If you have a child that is a scorekeeper, they may continually point out that one sibling may get more or less of something than the other, in terms of privileges, food, or just about anything else. They manipulate the situation into thinking you "favor" the other one over them. You may even find yourself justifying your decisions to them. If they're really good they may even convince you that indeed you do favor one child over another! Remember the guilt versus confident parent. Don't let them "guilt-you" into thinking this. What they may not realize is that perhaps one child gets more privileges because they've earned them. It goes back to freedom and independence. If a child is independent and for the most part does what is expected of them, then a natural consequence would be to grant them more freedom. When the other one argues that they weren't allowed to do that at their age you can explain this. At this point I do have to admit that we have always been more protective of our daughter because she is a girl and you just naturally worry more for girls' safety than for boys. This became more of an issue when she started driving. Even though she was a good kid that pretty much did what was expected of her, we still were more hesitant about her being out alone at night, than with our sons. On the other hand because she was a girl, I tended to buy her more clothes than her brothers because that was what she cared about. This is what I mean by "fair is not always equal".

Louanne Saenz

EXERCISE:
Think of a situation in your household where one child may have more of something than another. This could be something material, a particular privilege, or what is expected of them.

EXAMPLE: *We spend more on clothes for our daughter.*

1._____

2._____

3._____

Now write a reason for that particular decision. Can you honestly justify it?

EXAMPLE: *Because we spend more on hockey equipment for our son.*

Think about how you will explain it when a sibling questions your judgment.

VALUES

Values can be a controversial subject. Just about all parents feel they teach their kids values. In most cases this is true. The problem arises when family values are different from other families, or parents become territorial about who teaches those values. A good place to start is with our own country's **Core Democratic Values**. Here is a list with a simple definition from Michigan's Department of Education:

COMMON GOOD Help others at home and school

JUSTICE Take turns and be fair to others

LIBERTY Follow your beliefs and let others follow theirs

POPULAR SOVEREIGNITY Majority rules

LIFE Rules keep you safe, follow them

EQUALITY Give everyone an equal chance

DIVERSITY Work and play with everyone

PURSUIT OF HAPPINESS Have fun but follow the rules at home and school

TRUTH Tell the truth

PATRIOTISM Use core democratic values at home and school

RULE OF LAW Rules are made for everyone to follow

INDIVIDUAL RIGHTS We all have rights, but we should respect the rights of others as well.

As you can see these values are both general and specific enough not to cause too much controversy. Also keep in mind the saying, "It takes a village to raise a child." Children are constantly exposed to situations outside the home that will require discipline from others, particularly at school. While it may not be a school's major role to teach values, values will inevitably be taught by virtue of a different environment that demands rules and consequences for our actions. Sometimes the rules may even be slightly different than yours. For example, children get in trouble at school for fighting. Their explanation might be their parents told them if someone gave them a hard time they should defend themselves. While that advice may sound reasonable, their interpretation of that advice oftentimes is to punch the child that was giving them a hard time. It's one thing to do that in a neighborhood with a few kids nearby, and yet another in front of an entire class.

Kids need to learn that while the values may be consistent, the actions and rules used to carry out those values need to be adjusted, according to the environment. Allowing kids to learn that lesson early on is most valuable. If they are continually rescued from those types of situations, sooner or later they will learn them in another setting and the consequences may be considerably harsher. The point I am trying to make is to simply welcome the chance for children to learn limits and values from other settings, because that is how the world operates. We know that if we have ever worked for two different bosses.

In those isolated incidences where values do clash, hopefully a rational discussion can take place as to how to modify the situation so that all involved are satisfied.

Who Says Kids Don't Come With A Manual?

EXERCISE:

Reflect on the values you hold dear. Will they work in other settings besides your home? Why or why not?_____
_____
_____
_____

Louanne Saenz

WHO OWNS THE PROBLEM?

Sometimes situations arise that become problems for us, but not for our children. Messy rooms are a classic example of this. While that can drive us crazy, our kids couldn't care less. Unfortunately, the more we nag about it, the worse it gets. One of parenting's greatest challenges is transferring ownership to our kids. Until it interferes with something important to our children, it will never become their problem. How do we do that?

Finding the right opportunity and the leverage is the key. You will find some suggestions on the messy room dilemma under chores (section 5D). Sometimes we do deviate from our routines however. The opportunities that worked for me were when they would ask if they could go to a friend's house and I'd ask them if their room was done. If it wasn't then they simply cleaned it before I would take them there.

Morning routines are another time of frenzy in many households. We race around the house helping our children get ready, nagging them to hurry. They miss the bus and you have to drive them and consequently are late for work. Once again we know whose problem this is. In one of my parenting classes a mother came up with a creative solution to this problem. She had finally reached her limit so, very calmly, she told her kids that she could not drive them to school quite yet. They were mortified. They said they were going to be late and would have to get a tardy pass. (Now who owns the problem?) She went about her business and took them to school about ten minutes late. They hated it. After that, morning routines improved significantly!

Other options for transferring ownership with morning routines would be having them skip breakfast if they are running late. They can always grab a breakfast bar on the way to the bus. They won't starve, and if they are hungrier at lunch, they will remember that natural consequence. I have also suggested to parents that they send their child in pajamas, and pack their clothes. I'll admit that's a little easier to do if you are dropping them off at latch-key.

If you are going to change your routine like this, I would strongly suggest you tell them either that morning or the night before. Then stick to your promise. They may test you because they don't take you seriously. They may even get worse before they get better. That's actually a good sign! It means the transfer of ownership is beginning to take place!

Changing ownership boils down to a change in behavior on your part. Whatever the situation, it's obvious what is happening currently is ineffective. As I have stated before, change needs to begin with us. Waiting and hoping for our kids to change *before we do* is unrealistic. They have no motivation to change because they are getting what they want. We need to take the initiative and alter our approach and subsequent reaction.

If at this point you are thinking that there is really nothing your child cares about, think again! It is part of human nature to care. Have you come to a point in your relationship that your child says he doesn't care as a source of power over you? This type of behavior could be classified as passive-aggressive, and may require professional counseling.

The other question to ask yourself is if he doesn't care about anything could he be clinically depressed? If your child seems honestly indifferent about everything, you will also want to consider a professional opinion. A good place to start is your child's school. If the teacher notices the same thing, then pursue it further. If, on the other hand, he seems happy at school, then it's most likely either a power struggle with you or you just haven't found the right leverage yet.

Sometimes you discover the answer when you least expect it. Your child suddenly wants a new video game, or new outfit, and lately you have had it with his behavior. This would be a great opportunity to sit down calmly and have a heart-to-heart conversation with your child. You could express to him how you would love to get this for him, but lately you have been disappointed in him for whatever reason it happens to be. Then discuss with him, how to improve. DON'T say to him that if he improves, you will get him what he's just asked for. That is external motivation, in other words, you are motivating him to change his behavior for a reason other than the fact that it is the right thing to do. If he asks you once he improves, can he get some sort of reward, don't commit. You can always say you will reconsider at that point. (Motivation will be further explained in Section 4D.)

As long as you continue to assume ownership of your child's problem, whether it's taking their homework or lunch to school if they've forgotten it, or writing a note to the teacher because homework wasn't done, it will never become your child's problem. This isn't being mean; it's being realistic. We simply will not always be there to rescue them, and our children need to learn this early in life

This is all part of them becoming independent, earning freedom and privileges, and becoming self-confident as a result of doing their rightful share of daily tasks.

EXERCISE:

Think of a current situation in which YOU own the problem.

_____
_____
_____

Who Says Kids Don't Come With A Manual?

Now come up with a plan so that YOUR CHILD will own the problem.

_____
_____
_____

"REDUCE NOT ELMINATE"

"Reduce not eliminate" has to do with understanding that we will never eliminate problems in any household. A certain amount of conflict is healthy and inevitable. When you consider that your children go from being totally dependent to independent for the most part within an 18 to 20-year period, that has to lead to some type of growing pains. My point here simply is that if this manual can help you reduce the frequency of arguments then I have accomplished my goal.

EXERCISE:
During a typical week, how often would you say you argue with your children? Think about each child individually.

WEEK #1
Child #1. _____
Child #2. _____
Child #3. _____
Child #4. _____

WEEK #4
Child #1. _____
Child #2. _____
Child #3. _____
Child #4. _____

After a few weeks or so, do this again, and see if it's gotten better, worse or stayed the same. If things have gotten better, think of what it is you did differently. If things have gotten worse, what went wrong?
If things have stayed the same, ask yourself, "Have I done anything differently?"

"REPLACE NOT ERASE"

This is another saying I like to use. Think about a baby who has just discovered your keys, and is having a great time playing with them. Well it is now time to go and you need your keys. We all know that if we give him something else to replace the keys, hopefully distracting him, we have a much better chance of him not getting upset, as opposed to taking the keys away from him.

You can use this same principal in other situations. For example, your child has asked for a video game, which you feel is inappropriate for his age. A flat 'no' could create resentment. However if you suggested a different video, or better yet, a choice from two other videos, he may comply. Some persistent kids may insist on the original. That's always the fun part of parenting, standing firm, and praying you have the strength not to give in. The more often you offer an alternative, however, the less often they will argue.

This same principle can also apply to privileges. Maybe your child wants to stay out later than you are comfortable allowing. You could assure him that once he gets to a certain age (which hopefully is pretty soon) you will extend his curfew.

EXERCISE:
Think of a request that you know you will have to deny your child.
EXAMPLE: *Your child wants a new video game that is very costly.*

_____
_____
_____

Think of how you could respond with a "replacement" idea,

Louanne Saenz

rather than a flat "no."
EXAMPLE: *You would be willing to pay for half of it, or buy a less costly one.*

_____
_____
_____

YOU CAN MAKE A DIFFERENCE

Oftentimes parents, particularly mothers, would come to me concerned because they felt the other parent wasn't strict enough, or had lower expectations of their children than they did. This can be a frustrating situation. The truth of the matter is we can only control our own behavior. If you feel the other parent doesn't expect enough of your child, all hope is certainly not lost. In spite of their sometimes annoying qualities, children are resilient and intuitive. They know who lets them get away with more, and adjust their behavior to that situation. If you have a strong positive relationship with your child, you are going to have more influence. This can be the key to motivating your child whether it's a school issue or social issue.

Growing up, I had a mother who raised me with an iron hand, and a father who, while loving, was rather uninvolved when it came to my education. I knew there was no way, however, that I could get away with not working to my potential. This realization made a critical difference in my motivation to succeed. Even though my mother did demand a lot of me, we still had fun together. Sure there were times I thought she was unreasonable, but overall I knew she had my best interests at heart.

When you are concerned then, about your spouse or ex, stay focused on what you believe is the best for your child. I know this can be challenging, particularly in a divorce situation. One parent often feels the "heavy", because they do the homework with their children, get on them about limits and other issues. Just keep in mind that as long as you are finding bits of time for fun with your children, they will be able to accept your demands more easily. Remember influence, influence, influence!

The one exception I would make to this however, is even

Louanne Saenz

though you cannot control what goes on with an ex-spouse, if you feel your child is in danger, that's a totally different matter. Whether it's drugs, violence or neglect, action involving the courts or authorities needs to be taken. I know the court system doesn't always make it easy, but it will be worth the effort to keep your child safe. Once again this is how you can make a difference!

ZEROING IN ON THE ISSUE

I have said before that a significant part of this manual is self-evaluation and in so doing, be honest with yourself. Here is yet another chance to do this. Reflect on what some of your greatest issues are with your children. Now ask yourself why is this the case? While on the surface, it may sometimes appear that you are concerned about their well being, think again. Is part of the issue because you worry something could reflect negatively on you? This is a tough one. Most of us take pride in raising our children. When they turn out well, we would like to think it's at least somewhat of a reflection on us, and it truly is!

Let's take school for example, since kids spend so much time there. Do you take them their homework or lunch otherwise you think people will view you as a neglectful parent? I have had parents tell me that. When my sons were in elementary school, they had both put on shirts that looked like they had been slept in all night. Even though I told them my opinion, they really didn't care. I remember thinking that their teachers will assume I never iron. Even though I suggested they change, they didn't feel like it. Rather than argue, I just had to convince myself that if it didn't bother them, then it can't bother me. I did say that in the future however, if they were going out with me, then they would have wear something presentable. They reluctantly admitted that was fair enough.

As you reflect on the problems and issues you will inevitably encounter with your children, always be asking yourself why it's a problem for you. If you are worried about what others will think of you, versus ruining your relationship with your child, be careful. Haircuts and clothes come and go. They will survive once in a while without their lunch or homework. It's even all right to leave them at school kicking and screaming! They stop before you are barely to your car!

Louanne Saenz

Have confidence in yourself and don't let guilt scar your judgment!
EXERCISE:

Reflect on some of your greatest issues with your children. Do they revolve around what others will think? If so, what can you do about it?

_____
_____

Section 2:

BASIC HUMAN NEEDS

- A. **Behavior**
- B. **Fun**
- C. **Independence**
- D. **Love**
- E. **Power**

BEHAVIOR

Behavior is a very broad topic and overlaps many other subjects: discipline, communication, motivation, influence. The aspect of behavior I'd like to touch upon here is what *types of behavior are least tolerated*. All of us have our pet peeves. It would be very helpful for spouses to discuss this ahead of time, so that one parent doesn't undo the other parent's wishes. Psychiatrist and author of *Choice Theory*, William Glasser, explains that behavior stems from a motivation towards any one or all of five basic needs:

1. SURVIVAL: The need for the basics, food, clothing, shelter, and eventually, earning power
2. LOVE & BELONGING, Feeling a sense of ultimate love and trust with some**one**, (love) and a sense of comfort with various **groups** (belonging), i.e., extended families, classmates, various teams, church groups.
3. POWER, Feeling a sense of accomplishment, and being recognized for it.
4. FREEDOM, Being allowed age-appropriate choices and
5. FUN, being playful and enjoying a sense or discovery

EXERCISE:
Rank the types of needs and behaviors you differ about, on a scale of 1 to 5, 5 being "***Most Often differs***" to 1 being "***Least Often differs***" for each of your children over 2 years old.

Louanne Saenz

EXAMPLE:
CHILD #1:
Survival: 4
Love: 3
Power: 5
Freedom: 2
Fun: 1

Now pinpoint the issues, both negative (**differences**) and positive (*agreements*) for each category, beginning with Most Often (5)

EXAMPLE :
DIFFERENCES/ *AGREEMENTS*
5: POWER, never admits she's wrong, argues about anything, *Passionate and loyal, coming to other's defense when no one else will, says she's sorry*
4: SURVIVAL, Doesn't eat right, chores aren't regularly done, *makes & manages money very well*
3: LOVE, Thinks I favor her siblings more than her, *thoughtful and considerate most times, particularly on special occasions*
2: FREEDOM, Wants to go out too often on school nights, *obeys curfew*
1: FUN, Question choice of some friends, *enjoys what I like*

CHILD#2
Survival: 4
Love: 2
Power: 3
Freedom: 5
Fun: 1

Who Says Kids Don't Come With A Manual?

DIFFERENCES / *AGREEMENTS*
5: Freedom, Stays out past curfew,
Always lets me know where he is
4: Survival, Messy room,
makes and manages money very well
3: Power, Argues,
always does homework
2: Love, Says I hug him too much,
always comes to my defense
1: Fun, Plays Rap music too loud,
Doesn't let it interfere with school or work

CHILD #3
Survival: 5
Love: 1
Power: 4
Freedom: 3
Fun: 2

DIFFERENCES / *AGREEMENTS*
5: Survival: Messy, smelly room,
helps the most around the house
4: Power: Yells at me too much,
excellent student,
3: Freedom: Stays on computer too long,
obeys curfew
2: Fun: Plays on computer too much,
keeps it in perspective
1: Love: None,
Is wonderful to all relatives and adults.

Now it's your turn:

Louanne Saenz

CHILD #1
Survival: ____
Love: ____
Power: ____
Freedom: ____
Fun: ____

5: Difference_____

*Agreement*_____

4: Difference_____

*Agreement*_____

3: Difference_____

*Agreement*_____

2: Difference_____

*Agreement*_____

1: Difference_____

*Agreement*_____

Who Says Kids Don't Come With A Manual?

CHILD #2
Survival: ____
Love: ____
Power: ____
Freedom: ____
Fun: ____

5:Difference_____

*Agreement*_____

4:Difference_____

*Agreement*_____

3:Difference_____

*Agreement*_____

2:Difference_____

*Agreement*_____

1:Difference_____

*Agreement*_____

Louanne Saenz

CHILD #3
Survival: ____
Love: ____
Power: ____
Freedom: ____
Fun: ____

5: Difference_____

*Agreement*_____

4: Difference_____

*Agreement*_____

3: Difference_____

*Agreement*_____

2: Difference_____

*Agreement*_____

1: Difference_____

*Agreement*_____

Who Says Kids Don't Come With A Manual?

This exercise should demonstrate that your children aren't as bad as you think they are, or maybe it's confirmed that one of them is more or less of a problem than you thought. In either case, now return to the DIFFERENCE SIDE. Which differences do you feel so strongly about that there simply can't be a compromise? In our family it's church and homework. Church on Sunday was a given, regardless of extracurricular activities, as was homework. Our children knew that we would never write notes to their teachers excusing them from homework because of their schedules. This made them good time managers. On my part I was available to assist them if they were having trouble. Pretty much everything else was up for discussion.

Now go back and decide your non-negotiables, and ask yourself why indeed, are they non-negotiables? What are you willing to do to let your children understand this is the way it's going to be? Once you've decided, then it's time to make this clear to your children. Likewise also let them know that other topics are up for discussion. Doing it this way can effectively build relationships.

NOTE: If you truly struggled with the agreement side, and are top-heavy with the difference side, then your issues could be beyond the scope of this book. It may be the time to consider some outside counseling before it's too difficult to correct.

Louanne Saenz

EXERCISE:

List your two or three non-negotiables: (This will be the same for all your kids)

1._____

2._____

3._____

FUN

In this day and age of stress and busy schedules, fun is something we don't always have enough of, with our children. If you recall in the chapter on Behavior, Dr. William Glasser said that humans have 5 basic human needs, survival, love, freedom, power, and yes, fun. These needs are not equal with everyone, but with kids fun is high on THEIR list. Just to reiterate Glasser's definition of fun, it is the genetic instruction to be playful, to enjoy a sense of discovery.

For many years we heard the saying "quality not quantity" is what matters. Parents interpreted that to mean elaborate vacations or all day excursions, but that does not have to be the case at all!! Fun can be as simple as playing cards together, going for ice-cream or bedtime reading. I remember a student saying all she wanted to do was play cards with her mother one night because she hardly ever saw her. The mother was shocked that such a simple activity meant so much to her child. These will be the memories your children will cherish forever. Be wary of the phrase, "I'm too busy." Think of these times as an investment of your time and not an expense. You will reap a thousand fold in benefits and "warm fuzzies" as you bond with your child.

The other type of fun Glasser refers to is the fun that comes from learning something new (discovery). Remember when you first learned how to ride a bike? You probably took a few spills, scraped your knee, but then finally got the hang of it. Once you learned how to do it, it became fun.

Teaching your child to do something fun can be a great bonding experience. This is particularly true for boys. William Pollack, psychologist and author of **Real Boys**, suggests doing things with boys as a way of bonding and helping them open up. His sessions would be at the local fishing hole, because he discovered that boys talk more when they are doing something, rather than sitting face to face. A little caution here is sometimes what we think of as fun, may not necessarily be fun for your child. I love to cook, yet none of my children have shown any interest in that. If your child does express an interest in learning to do something you are good at, by all means, take advantage of that situation. We have so much we can teach our children, whether it's sewing, playing a sport or game, or computer skill. What a feeling it is when we pass our knowledge on to our kids and watch them excel.

A favorite fun bedtime activity we used to enjoy was taking turns talking about our day. We would take turns finishing the phrase, "I liked it when" or "it was fun when". Some of my best memories with my kids were from this little exercise.

Just remember, fun is what you make it. It doesn't have to be expensive or extremely time-consuming. As Nike says, "Just do it"!!

EXERCISE:

Think of two or three fun, cheap activities that both you and your child enjoy doing together. Figure out which can be done on a daily, weekly or monthly basis.

EXAMPLE:

DAILY: *Reading at bedtime*
WEEKLY: *Renting a video, scrap-booking, watching them play a sport, bike-riding*
MONTHLY: *Going to a fast food joint together, clothes shopping*

YOUR TURN:
DAILY: _____
WEEKLY: _____

Who Says Kids Don't Come With A Manual?

MONTHLY:_____

If you are thinking that you don't have time to do this, analyze your priorities. Children need this time and once again, if you don't invest in positive time with your child, you will risk spending negative time on nagging, blaming and criticizing.

Louanne Saenz

INDEPENDENCE

Independence is an under-rated commodity. Parents tend to stifle this attribute, consequently affecting their child's self-confidence. If we do want to boost our children's self-confidence, teaching independence is a very effective way to do this. Whenever I ask parents about how to boost their child's confidence, the two most common responses are, having good friends and family support, and good grades or some other type of achievement example. Independence rarely, if ever, gets mentioned. Being independent, is the third leg of the self-confidence stool, along with love and achievement. Independence leads to healthy initiative and healthy risk-taking.

Independence goes hand in hand with freedom. Remember the Revolutionary War, otherwise known as the War of Independence. What were we fighting for? Our freedom! Do you remember the sense of satisfaction you had when you could dress yourself, or drive or make your own money? It was very fulfilling. Children need that feeling too in order to grow and develop.

I'm reminded of a story about an egg that began to hatch. The mother was so excited when she heard her offspring pecking to break free, that she helped it along. But when she broke open the egg her little baby withered and died. You see the chick need the strengthening exercise of hatching on its own in order to strengthen its own body. Without that, it simply wasn't strong enough to survive on its own. Children need those little exercises too in order to gain confidence for their own successful future.

Parents seem to be all over the board on this subject however. I've seen first- graders come to school having to do everything from getting their own breakfast and lunch because mom won't get up, to first graders coming to school expecting to be fed! Obviously we need to be somewhere in between. If you have more than one child, you may notice that one just may be more naturally independent. Think about the message you are sending when you constantly do for your child. It's one of two things. Either "It's just faster if I do it," because I'm too impatient to teach you myself, or "You can't do this, it's too dangerous or you're not capable of doing it." I don't know about you, but I wouldn't want my child to be thinking those things.

At this point it may be helpful to list by age, appropriate independent tasks for your child.

One: Walking
Two: Potty train, feed themselves
Three: Begin to dress themselves
Four: Master dressing themselves
Five: Zip jacket, tie shoes, button clothes, walk to classroom alone
Six: Getting simple breakfast
Seven: Making lunches w/ help, doing homework
Eight: Ride bike to friend's house if on side street, using microwave
Nine/Ten: Begin babysitting training during day for short periods
Eleven/Twelve: Using stove with supervision
Thirteen: Babysitting longer, i.e. evenings
Fourteen-Seventeen: Driving, cooking, getting a job
Eighteen: You've raised a pretty self-sufficient young person!

This is definitely not an all-inclusive list. In fact feel free to add to it. I did not include chores at this point because we will be covering them later.

CAUTION: If you find yourself disagreeing with the list because you think they're not ready, could you be one of those parents, parenting expert, Jim Fay, calls "Helicopters", because you're always hovering over your child? On the other hand, if you can add a lot more to the list, are you expecting too much? Remember if we want our children to be accurate self-evaluators, we need to begin and be honest with ourselves!!!

Earlier I said that independence and freedom go hand in hand. Let me explain. If your child does his homework without reminders, occasionally baby-sits his sibs without a problem, and pretty much follows household rules, are you going to be more apt to agree to a slightly later curfew or other privileges he might be requesting? I would venture to say that his request would more likely be open to discussion if this is the case. That's what I mean by independence and freedom going hand in hand. The more independent your child proves to be, the more likely you would trust him with more freedom. This concept isn't always that obvious to kids however. You need to explain this logic to them, so they understand the responsibility that's required in order to earn more freedom. I must say it will make sense to your kids, and can go a long way in motivating them to become more independent and capable. It's a great negotiating item when you can say to them, "I'll be happy to let you stay out a half-hour later, when you show me that you can get your homework done without my nagging you to get started."

Who Says Kids Don't Come With A Manual?

EXERCISE:
Think of something your child has been asking to do that involves more freedom. Now think of an independent task you have been expecting of him that you could discuss and turn into a win/win situation for both of you.

Freedom Request: (Child's) EXAMPLE: *Curfew extended half an hour on weekends*

_____
_____
_____
_____

Independence Request: (Parent's) EXAMPLE: *Have all independent homework completed by the time parents come home from work*

_____
_____
_____
_____

Louanne Saenz

LOVE

Ah, the things we do for love! How often do we do things for our children and justify it in the name of love. Our hearts are in the right place, but is that truly helping our kids? The goal of this section is once again to help us self-evaluate our actions as parents. At what point does something stop being a loving action and instead become an enabling action? I know of numerous occasions where parents would bring their children's homework or lunch to school because their child had forgotten it. These weren't isolated times but regular happenings, done in the name of love. Talk about sabotaging their child's behavior. All they learned from this was, "I don't have to worry about my homework or lunch because mom will bring it for me. Kids do survive without lunch or an assignment once in a while. They will more likely to remember it in the future if you don't rescue them, and it becomes their problem much sooner. This can be very liberating for you too! If we truly want to foster our children's self-confidence, then we need to back off on occasions and let them make some small mistakes. This is true love. Sooner or later, whether we like it or not, we need to take the training wheels off the bike and let them ride on their own.

Helping our kids grow up into self-sufficient adults is a bittersweet process. While it feels good to be needed, it's also rewarding to watch them stand on their own feet. We also have to realize that before they stand however they may stumble and fall in the process.

I haven't mentioned this yet, but two and a half years ago, I was diagnosed with breast cancer. It was the scariest time of my life. I had to endure painful surgeries, chemotherapy and radiation, the whole nine yards. I am happy to say that so far I am cancer free and I feel great. Had I not endured that suffering in order to be cured, however, I may not be here today to write this book. My point simply is that we can't use the excuse that we love our children too much to let them suffer. For some kids, the only way they do learn is through the school of "hard knocks" while other kids learn by a simple warning. The earlier they learn from their mistakes, while the stakes are still small, the less they will suffer in the long run.

A point I learned the hard way was that while I was pretty comfortable letting my kids learn from their own small mistakes, I could sometimes go overboard in accommodating their schedules at the expense of my own. I honestly thought that was the loving thing to do. My rationale for this was if I set the right example for them, they will learn to do the same in return. It didn't work that way however. What they learned was simply that Mom was always there at a moment's notice to be their chauffeur. The light finally went on one day, and I realized that for them to learn to be accommodating, they had to accommodate my schedule so they understood the give and take of relationships. Once I rose above the guilt (there's that "G" word again!) of saying "No," they learned to be more aware of other's feelings and expectations, and consequently become more loving, caring children.

Louanne Saenz

EXERCISE:

Think of something you are doing in the name of love that is actually an enabling behavior. EXAMPLE: (*I constantly yell for them to wake up*).

_____
_____
_____
_____

Now replace that behavior with another action. EXAMPLE: (*I will get them an alarm clock, and if they're late they can deal with it in school*).

_____
_____
_____
_____

POWER

As you will recall, earlier I said that according to psychiatrist, William Glasser, Power is one our basic human needs. In fact many psychological theories include power as one of man's basic needs. Freud called it aggression, Adler and Dreikers call it power, just to name a few. Glasser however splits power into two categories. He calls one type "power over" as in bossing and controlling others; and the other as "personal power," the power derived from achievement and being recognized for that achievement.

The first type of power, "power over" is what most parents fight about with their kids. Remember, just as too much or not enough attention results in attention getting behavior, so it is with power. Where this gets tricky is determining how much power is appropriate for our kids, since they, just as we, have differing power needs.

Referring back to the section on behavior, and the exercise you did, is "power over" a major problem with ALL of your children? Then it may be your issue. If it is only a problem with one of your children, then it may be more their need. Remember I said this manual is about self-evaluating. You need to be honest with yourself before you can begin to solve problems with your children.

I was in a second grade classroom when we were discussing the meanings of power. I asked which students were allowed to choose what they wore to school most mornings. All the students raised their hand except for one child. That particular child was always getting in trouble for bullying and other power-related behaviors. That one answer was a real eye-opener. It confirmed the fact that if parents try to micro-manage all decisions, it could result in excessive power driven behaviors elsewhere. School, in particular would offer many opportunities for power issues to surface.

So, what power-over issues are the major sources of conflict in your family? It's one thing to fight over a haircut that grows back in a month. It's a whole other matter to argue about girl or boyfriends. Although the following may sound like a contradiction, keep this in mind: The more power or control you are willing to relinquish to your child, at least in small matters, the more control you will recoup in larger matters. Again think of this as an investment, not an expense. Every time you "deposit" some power to your child, it makes it easier to "withdraw" power from them in situations that really matter. Choose your power battles carefully. Remember your non-negotiables? Have you stuck with those, or do you keep randomly adding or subtracting from the list?

Another extremely important point to keep in mind is consistency with your spouse about power-over issues. In many households one parent may be stricter than the other and children will figure that out quickly. This can be very confusing to them. As you may have noticed, I don't give too many "nevers" but I will state one here. NEVER undo what the other parent has already decided. You are setting yourself up for a lot of conflict. If you do disagree with your spouse over some decision, then discuss it privately. If one of you changes your mind, then you can simply say so to your child, after discussing it with the other parent. If, on the other hand, the decision is NOT to allow them to do something they've requested, when one parent already said it was OK, I don't have to tell you what will happen next. I love my husband's line in these situations. When one of our kids asked him something, and he wasn't sure, he simply asked, "What did Mom say?" He thought of that on all by himself! I don't mean to imply that I make the decisions in our household; it's just that I tend to worry and think of problems that could arise, ones that don't always occur to him. By asking them "What did Mom say?" the answer is delayed, and we presented a united front, which effectively diffuses

Who Says Kids Don't Come With A Manual?

many power struggles. Even if you are separated, you can always say you are going to call the other parent and talk to them before you make a decision. This would be particularly helpful if the decision you make is going to impact the children's actions.

The other aspect of power I want to briefly discuss is "personal" power. What Glasser means by this is the power we derive from mastering a skill and being recognized for it. When was the last time you mastered something new? What did that feel like? I don't know about you, but I find that feeling very satisfying. In fact once you have mastered that skill, it becomes fun, and consequently intrinsically rewarding.

We need to notice those improvements in our children and acknowledge them, no matter how small, particularly if they have been struggling for a while. If we wanted to lose 40 pounds and no-one said anything until we lost 35 pounds, it would be harder to persevere. Children need the same encouragement. They derive "personal power" from knowing you notice when they can add or subtract in their heads versus using their fingers, for example. The more we acknowledge these small improvements, lets them know you care, and is yet another relationship builder.

Louanne Saenz

EXERCISE:

What issues do you get into power struggles most often with your children?
EXAMPLE: *Going out on a school night.*

1. _____

2. _____

3. _____

A. Which of these *are* negotiable ?

B. Choose one and describe how you would negotiate a resolution with your child.
EXAMPLE: "*You can go out on a school night, **after** I see proof that homework (non-negotiable) is complete. Your curfew will be_____.*

Section 3:

COMMUNICATING WITH OUR CHILDREN:

- A. Empathy
- B. Emotional Intelligence
- C. Humor
- D. Messages
- E. No!
- F. Praise vs. Encouragement
- G. Questioning
- H. Quiet
- I. Remorse
- J. Rehearse
- K. "Rewind the Video"
- L. Expectations
- M. Example
- N. "You Have to Try It. You Don't Have to Like It."
- O. Talking to Your Children (Summary)

EMPATHY

Simply stated, empathy is "putting yourself in another person's shoes." This applies to parenting when your child comes to you upset or disappointed about something and you say something like, "oh that's no big deal", "you'll get over it", or worse yet, you give an example of how things were even worse than that for you one time. Your child just wants acknowledgement of his feelings. If he's just lost a championship game, he has a right to be disappointed. Let him know that's justified. It's not necessary to go into a lecture as to what he could have done differently. Would you want to hear advice from someone, just after you'd found out you'd been overlooked for a promotion? Chances are you'd want someone to say something like "Yeah, it must be hard not getting that promotion. You're a great worker." Kids want the same thing. All too often we find ourselves offering advice instead of consolation, implying that they should shove their feelings under the carpet.

When my son was in fourth grade, he happened to be absent the day of student council elections. He went back to school the next day, only to find out that someone else had won. He was devastated. He wanted me to speak to his teacher, which I did the following day, since it happened to be Conference Day. What he'd hoped I had done, though, was ask the teacher to hold another election. Well that wasn't going to happen. There really wasn't anything else I could do for him. I felt so helpless just holding him and saying it was too bad he was absent that day. Sure enough the next morning, he'd bounded out of bed, having totally gotten over it. I'm sure if I'd said to get over it, or better luck next year, he would have still been stewing about it the next day.

At this point I do want to qualify the empathy scenario. Some children can be melodramatic about *everything*. If you put the wrong cookies in their lunch, or they get a B instead of an A, they don't have to go into hysterics, even though we know some kids will. Everyday situations like these call for a simple apology, a suggestion to pack their own lunch, or discussing what they could do to earn an A. Situations calling for a higher level of empathy are the times that occur less regularly. Competitive situations, for example, where they took the risk to try out for something, a commendable feat in itself, and they lost, be it a sport, musical part, or election. You can respond empathetically with, "It must be hard not to make it after how much you practiced." Later it could be followed by what they could do for future tryouts.

Other times calling for more empathy are when your child is left out of something such as not being invited to a party. Those are difficult times as parents. Your first instinct is to call the decision maker and just tell them off. I don't have to tell you that that only embarrasses your child further. Some kids though, may ask their parents to do just that. My suggestion would be to talk to your child about why they think they might not have been invited, and see if the reason is something that is in or out of their control. Then they could figure out what to do to increase their opportunities for future invitations.

A final note on empathy: Sometimes all we can do is be there for our children. We live in a "fix-it" society, but sometimes "fixing it" isn't an option. Letting them have a good cry over their disappointment and agreeing that it's tough not to make it, or be left out is all we can do, and is really all they are looking for. Just ask them! I know I did, and the response was always the same, "Thanks Mom, but there's nothing you can really do". They're right, so just be there for them. It definitely reduces the healing time and should hopefully make them better able to handle future disappointments which we know that they will inevitably face.

EMOTIONAL INTELLIGENCE
("People Smarts")

Throughout a child's school career, intelligence, aptitude, ability, is always emphasized and highly esteemed. Yet we know many capable students who fail, don't work up to capacity or simply don't care. On the other hand we know of average students who work their little hearts out, have a great attitude and whom everyone loves. That's because the latter group possesses EMOTIONAL intelligence (E.Q.), a rather new term coined by author Daniel Goleman. In fact emotional intelligence (E.Q.) the ability to:
a) understand oneself and b) get along with others, is proving to be a greater indicator of success than I.Q.

We all know of people who are highly intelligent and are either unemployed, cannot maintain a satisfying relationship, or are just plain miserable. On the contrary we also know of people who might not have had the highest ACT or SAT scores yet go on to be highly successful both personally and professionally, once again because of their emotional intelligence or what I like to call "people smarts."

What does this have to do with child-rearing? A lot! The good news is that emotional intelligence (EQ) is not as "set" as intelligence (IQ). A window of opportunity exists during childhood and adolescence to actually change the brains' neural pathways and improve your child's EQ. or "people smarts" in many instances, by the type of questions you ask your child.

To state it simply, emotional intelligence has two components:

1) **Understanding oneself**, which also includes controlling emotions and motivating oneself.

2) ***Getting along with others***, which also includes empathy.

Understanding oneself is the ability to honestly self-evaluate one's own ***behavior and achievement*** so as to properly motivate oneself. The challenge in this is that children are so used to being measured and evaluated by ***others***, that they don't learn how to evaluate themselves. As parents we can begin to train them by the questions we ask. Simple questions such as, "*Do you think you've gotten better, worse or stayed the same?*" (this can apply to a sport, subject, or more importantly, their own behavior) Always follow it up by " *How do you know?*" Have them be specific! Another question is, "*Was this too easy, too hard or just right?*" *How can you tell?* (This can apply to their report card, a book they're reading, an assignment or any other skill or project.)
"*How do you think you did?*" *How do you know?*"
I hope you get the idea of this type of questioning. The point is to have ***them*** be able to explain their answer to you.

I do this exercise even with first graders. It's amazing how some students naturally know how to self-evaluate while others don't have a clue. If your child doesn't have a clue when you ask for proof of their answer, you can always ask them some leading questions in the beginning, until they get better at it. For example if you're trying to find out if they think they've become a better reader and they say they don't know, you could ask them to show you books they can read now versus ones from the beginning of the school year.

Sometimes children claim they don't know if they've improved as a way of getting out of admitting they haven't. That needs to be questioned the same way as documenting improvement, always making them explain their answer. American children have developed a notorious reputation for having such high self-esteem while rating low on standardized tests. While we don't want our children to become suicidal over this matter, as in some cultures, we do want them to strike a good balance in knowing what they are both proficient in and what needs improvement.

How often should you do this? This depends on their age. The younger they are, the more often you may want to check this out, in order to give them enough practice at self-evaluating. A good opportunity to do this is just before report cards. It would be easy to find out if they think their grades are going to be higher, lower, or the same. You could write it down and then compare their answers when they actually get the report cards. Some teachers actually give their students a blank report card for the kids to fill out, then compare it to the actual one. If your child's teacher does this, request a copy of it.

The other component of emotional intelligence is ***getting along with others***. We all remember the kids that always had so many friends, were easy to talk to or could always make you laugh. We also know the loners, and the kids people feared. What you want to make sure of, is that your child is happy and comfortable with his friendship status.

Some kids prefer to have one best friend and not much more. Others prefer lots of friends. Take your cue from your child. If they genuinely seem happy with one best friend (as I was), then let it go. Many parents worry about this. If on the other hand, your child is complaining that they don't have any friends, then that naturally needs to be investigated. I hate to say this, but in most cases, not having enough friends is often their own fault. Again through self-evaluation, driven by the questions you ask regarding friendships, hopefully they will come to the conclusion that part of it is their fault and they need to work on their own behavior, because that is what they can control. Handling relationships then, will improve and ultimately so will their emotional intelligence!

Louanne Saenz

HUMOR

Living in Michigan, we are prone to snow storms that dump twelve inches in a very short time, rendering traffic to a crawl. After one particular storm, my typical fifteen minute drive took an hour. I was almost home when my youngest son, Carl called asking me to pick him up from a friend's house. Mind you, the friend lived walking distance from my job and I could have easily picked him up on my way home. I pulled in to a parking lot calling home, my son, and my husband, yelling at all of them. In that state of mind, I had to drive all the way back from where I came. I remember telling my son to sit in the back seat, because I didn't want to look at him, I was so disgusted. All parenting rationale was out the window. By the way, he was fifteen at the time and should have known better. When we arrived home my husband sent Carl back out to shovel the snow from the driveway, and called my older son home from another friend's house saying, "You better come **now,** and ***expect conflict***." When my oldest son arrived home, upon meeting Carl at the drive way was told, "Don't bother going in the house, just start shoveling snow." On seeing both sons shoveling, my husband jokingly said, "When you're finished shoveling the snow, put it all back and then shovel it again."

Humor, like fun, is an under-rated, under-used commodity. I know I am guilty of forgetting about it. As you can see, my husband, on the other hand has a gift for interjecting it, at just the right moments. We can all look back on that story now and have a good laugh together about it.

If you or your spouse is blessed with a sense of humor, by all means use it every chance you get. It diffuses so any arguments, thus leading to a more peaceful resolution. I love parenting expert, Jim Fay's, one-liners, like "I love you too much to argue", or "Nice try". At school when kids are getting a little too silly I'll say, "It sounds like you're having too much fun,"

Who Says Kids Don't Come With A Manual?

and they usually get the idea.

You may already know that when we laugh it releases powerful mood boosters called endorphins into our systems. Remember the movie *Patch Adams*, the story of the famous physician who used humor in his interaction with patients? Humor can promote physical and mental health. While recovering from my surgery, and to help me endure chemotherapy, I watched comedies on T.V. regularly, and rented funny movies. This is another easy way to spend time with your kids. I remember vividly, when my children were very young, the first time I would hear them cackle with laughter at cartoons, or appreciate funny scenes, in various sit-coms. To me it was priceless. Never under-estimate the power of humor. It can be your most valuable asset in times of need. Our children still laugh about the time they found their shoes on the deck, because my husband was tired of tripping over them.

EXERCISE:

Come up with 2 or 3 one-liners you can tell your kids to avoid an argument.

    1. _____
    2. _____
    3. _____

Louanne Saenz

MESSAGES

This is another topic I enjoy sharing with you because of something I read years ago. In the book *Kids Can Cooperate*, Elizabeth Crary discusses two types of messages we send our children:

BEING MESSAGES: are *Unearned* messages we say at any time about how much we love them. They tend to be pretty generic. "I love you", "You're the best" and so on. They are said spontaneously.

DOING MESSAGES: are *Earned* messages we send our children in response to some type of accomplishment. "Wow all A's! Fantastic! "Your room looks great!" These are better given privately, and not in front of another sibling, so as not to create any resentment.

As parents we may tend to say more of one type of message than the other. Of course the goal is striking a balance. If you only send "being" messages, the child may feel he can do no wrong. If you only send "doing" messages, your child may think that you only care about them when they accomplish something, and worry about the withdrawal of your love if they don't make the mark. Be aware of what messages you give on a given day, and make an effort to use both.

"I" MESSAGES: are used any time, particularly when we are upset. The **"I" message formula** is:

"**I feel** _____ **when you** _____ **because** _____.

Please _____."

I personally have trouble with the "I feel" part, so I've tweaked my version to be "<u>I get</u>" _____ "<u>when you</u>" etc. The advantage with "I" messages is when you begin a sentence with the word "I" it will tend to be less demeaning. Oftentimes when we begin with the word "You", the next thing that comes out of our mouths is some type of name or dramatic insult that we later regret saying. "I" messages may be tough to come up with in the midst of anger. Again strive for improvement not perfection. If you've never used them, you can only get better!

UNSPOKEN MESSAGES: are delivered by how we *act* and what we might *not* say. It's been said that human communication is 20% verbal and 80% non-verbal. Actions *do* speak louder than words. If we are still walking our children to their classroom when no one else is, or driving them to school when others are walking or riding the bus, the unspoken message here is "You are not capable of doing this yourself." Oftentimes, unspoken messages relate to independence issues. Most of us would not *say* "You can't do this" or "I have to do this for you," but the message still appears that way. Some parents claim it's often simpler to do things themselves rather than invest time trying to teach their child. That's probably true, but how are they going to learn if we don't take the time to teach them?

What about the child who insists you do drive them to school because someone is mean to them on the bus. Be sure to check out the facts first. In most cases it is an exaggerated perception on your child's part. Again the message you need to send is that your child is capable of doing this himself. If, in fact, someone is giving them a hard time, meet with the principal and determine an appropriate course of action.

Louanne Saenz

EXERCISE:

Think of a "**BEING**" message you can say to your child spontaneously,
EXAMPLE: *"I love you,"* or *"You are my sunshine"*
_____.

Now think of a couple specific "**DOING**" messages you can say to your child.

EXAMPLE: *"Thanks for remembering to make your bed".*
1._____
2._____

Use the "I Message" formula to tell your child about something that has upset you.
EXAMPLE: **I feel** (worried) **when you** (don't call that you'll be late) **because** (I think something's happened to you) **Please** (remember to call next time)

I feel _____ **when you** _____ **because** _____.
Please_____.

NO!

How often do we find ourselves uttering this little word? Do we say it a lot, perhaps as a means of gaining some power OVER our kids, or rarely because we are afraid our kids will get mad at us or not like us. Obviously we want to strive for some type of balance, but easier said than done.

Consider your reason for saying "no." If you say it a lot, are you into control, or possibly thinking, "I never questioned my parents, why should they question me?" Fortunately or not, that just isn't good enough for today's kids. Most answers do require some type of explanation. On the other hand, are you hesitant to say no because your kids will get upset with you and manipulate you into thinking you're mean. I know that is what I often thought. So how do you attain a happy medium?

Try this technique. When children ask you to do something with which you have a problem, there are several options:

1. You can ask them something like, "Do you think I should let you?"(Watch your tone of voice) If you have a charismatic child whom you know will come up with some charming answer, be ready and respond with, "Nice try", and then explain your concerns.

2. If you feel strongly about not letting them do something, you can soften it with an explanation for your answer. This may not stop the arguing, but it will not damage the relationship as much either.

3. If you're not sure, then don't give an answer right away. Simply explain that you need to think about it or discuss it with their father.

4.   If it is a situation that requires an immediate reply, and you're just not sure, say no to that particular time, but then explain that next time they need to give you more notice, and you would reconsider. Kids like that "hope" for the future and know that you can be flexible.

So much of this manual is about self-reflection, be it our own or our children's. If the request is a first time request, I would be asking myself, why should I let them? If you think back to the section on independence, we said that freedom and independence go hand-in-hand. I'm sure that many of the times that require yes or no answers have to do with freedom issues. As a guideline, then, consider how independent and responsible your child is up to this point and base your answer on that.

When my daughter was a senior, she asked me if she could go to the midnight premier of "Star Wars" on a school night. My immediate response would have leaned toward a "no", but as I thought about it, since she was a good student, thought it was all right. I made it very clear that I would not write a note to let her go to school late the next morning. As long as she could get up the next day for school, I said "yes." If she had given me a hard time about it, she could forget ever asking me something like that again. Well, she did go to the movie, she got up for school the next day, and all went well. I also had made sure she didn't have any important exams.

Times like this are also opportunities to deliver negative content messages with a positive relationship message. Express your sincere regret that you have to say "no" this time because of whatever capabilities they haven't proven themselves, but that they have your word that as soon as they display improvement in that area, the freedom bar will get lifted too!

Who Says Kids Don't Come With A Manual?

EXERCISE:

Think of a time you said "No" when you either could have said "Yes," or at least given a reason for your answer.

_____
_____
_____

Now think of a time you said "Yes" when you should have said "No". How can you get more confident for next time?

_____
_____
_____

Louanne Saenz

PRAISE vs. ENCOURAGEMENT

We've just talked about noticing improvement in our kids. How do you usually communicate that to your child? The most common line I hear is "I'm so proud of you!" While this is always said with the best of intentions, this is a trite example of praise. So what's wrong with that? While there is nothing wrong with praise, what we really want to strive for is encouragement.

Jim Fay does an excellent job of distinguishing between praise and encouragement. To summarize his thoughts: Praise is often quite general. Encouragement is more specific. For example, "Wow, 85%! That's quite an improvement!"

Praise often refers to your own feelings. Encouragement recognizes their feelings. "You must feel really good about that B", or "Your hard work sure paid off!" Now don't go ruining it by adding, "I told you, you could do it!" as I used to do! That's just another form of "I told you so", and you know how we all hated hearing that as a child. Think about your own work situation. Wouldn't it sound a little strange if your boss said to you, "Great job! I'm so proud of you!" How much more encouraging is it if he says, "Thanks for handling that situation. I know it was uncomfortable for you. You took care of it very professionally."

Praise is often judgmental, while encouragement is descriptive. "What a good boy"(praise) can be replaced by, "*I noticed you let her go first.*"

Who Says Kids Don't Come With A Manual?

EXERCISE:
Think of some phrases you say now, that are more like praise, or close to it.
Now how can you tweak them to sound more encouraging?

EXAMPLE: Replace "great job!" (praise) with *"You must feel really good about that!"*, or *"Your hard work paid off!"* or *"That extra practice really showed up in today's game!"* (Then give an example of what they did)

Feel free to use the above, then create one or two of your own.
_____
_____

Louanne Saenz

QUESTIONING

Lecturing our children is a habit all parents have. With just a little practice, however, that scolding can be rephrased into questions. As a counselor I have the advantage of being able to do this just about every day. It's a great way to help kids figure out for themselves if they're about to make a mistake or not. For example, your child storms in after just having had a fight with a friend. A common temptation is to side with your child, or offer advice such as calling another friend to play. Instead try this scenario.

Parent: What happened?
Child: So-and-so always has to have his way.
Parent: What do you mean?
Child: He said that if I don't go to the park, he won't be my friend.
Parent: Why didn't you want to go to the park?
Child: That's all we ever do. I wanted to go to so-and-so's house instead.
Parent: Why didn't he want to go there?
Child: I don't know. He says he doesn't like him.
Parent: Could he be worried about being left out when you play with him?
Child: I don't know.
Parent: Did you ask him?
Child: Well, no.
Parent: Do you think that might be a good idea?
Child: I guess so.
Parent: When do you plan on doing this?

I think you get the idea. Of course there are certainly other questions you could ask. Eventually, however you want to get to a question that will lead to some kind of action on your

Who Says Kids Don't Come With A Manual?

child's part.

When I am counseling students who have had arguments at school, I always seem to get to the question, "Did you ask him why he did whatever it was that he had done?" Invariably they answer "No." For the most part, they usually admit that would be a good idea. I get a commitment from them as to when they will do this. Sometimes you might need to role play with your child and help them develop the conversation. Then ask them how it went to see if they need to come up with a different plan.

EXERCISE:

Think of a situation(s) that comes up repeatedly with your child, that often upsets him. This could be in a school or social setting.

_____
_____
_____
_____
_____

How can you formulate some of your statements as questions?

_____
_____
_____
_____
_____

Louanne Saenz

QUIET

The cliché "Silence is Golden" can go a long way in child-rearing. Although it takes some self-control, sometimes silence is more effective than arguing. Those stressful times when I knew I was about to be insulting and degrading, I would be quiet. Eventually my kids got the message that this was my way of letting them know I had had it. They said nothing either and at least we didn't regret as much later on, when we could sit down and discuss it more rationally.

Another technique I used when I was upset about their behavior, I would warn them to get out of my sight before I said or did anything I would regret. This of course meant going to their room, not out the door. They usually scrammed pretty fast!

REMORSE

Remorse is a subject that easily gets overlooked. Sure we want kids to be sorry for what they did, but more often than not, they are sorry because of the punishment they are going to get, and not for what they did to someone. At school, every single time a child was crying for winding up in the principal's office, I would ask why they were crying. Every time, they answered because their parents were going to ground them or use some other punishment. I would always have to dig deeper to get them to regret what they had done for more mature reasons. Granted, part of this is age and maturity. However, we can't expect kids to suddenly become remorseful on their own.

Early on children don't realize that their actions can have a negative impact on someone else. They are too busy thinking about the consequences. Oftentimes the logical or related consequence that needs to occur is a direct apology either written or spoken. You might think, "Is that all? That's not enough." I can tell you that every time a victim is called in to receive an apology, it is delivered with regret and embarrassment. In fact the victim sometimes feels badly, because he didn't realize how guilty the other person felt. This is one of those wonderful moments when children learn and understand the consequences of their actions. Remorse, then, is a forerunner to helping children empathize. Their consequent feelings of regret will hopefully lead to thinking through and preventing similar future mistakes.

EXERCISE:

Think of a situation that happens repeatedly that you would like your child to be more remorseful about.

EXAMPLE: *He calls his little brother "stupid" when he has*

Louanne Saenz

trouble with his homework.

_____
_____
_____

What can you say to help him feel remorseful about saying that?

EXAMPLE: *Have him first apologize and if he knows how, have him help his brother with his homework*

_____
_____
_____

REHEARSE

I'm sure certain situations occur repeatedly. Anticipating those times can be critical in effectively handling them. It is somewhat of a "surprise" tactic. Your kids will be "thrown off" by the fact that you saw this behavior coming and addressed it ***before*** it happened. For example, you are taking your preschooler grocery shopping with you. Previous times he's asked for everything in sight, and has a tantrum if he doesn't get it. This time before you even get in the car, make it clear that he may request just one item. You might even determine the item before you leave, stressing that any other requests or whining will result in no treat. You can also perk up the situation by telling them, they ***can*** help choose various items, like favorite cereal or ice-cream.

Another situation where anticipating/rehearsing is useful would be any subjects which often lead to arguments. Perhaps you and your daughter don't see eye-to-eye on the value of good grades. Hence, report card time is always dreaded. Before report cards come home, think in your mind how you are going to most tactfully approach the situation. Rehearse it in your mind. Write it down if that helps. I used to practice in the car, when I was driving to and from work.

Louanne Saenz

EXERCISE:

Think of a situation(s) that repeatedly occurs with your child(ren)

1._____

2._____

3._____

Now write down what you are going to say and rehearse it.

1._____

2._____

3._____

"REWIND THE VIDEO"

This is a favorite saying of mine and I use it often with children when they are in trouble. I simply ask them to pretend the entire situation was on video. Then I ask them to rewind the video to where the trouble started. They understand the metaphor and are honest enough and able to tell me where the trouble began. Then I ask them what they could have done differently so that the story could either have a happy ending, or so that they wouldn't have gotten in trouble. I cannot think of one situation where the child was not able to think of a different ending. It works very well.

Another advantage of this technique is that you are taking the focus away from their mistakes of the past and replacing it with success for future situations. Too often people get hung up on why didn't they think of this or that and the conflict gets deeper and deeper. With this technique, children are provided with tools to prepare them for re-occurrence. Your kids will know that you are honestly trying to help them and this further cements your relationship. Keep in mind that this will be more effective in less severe situations, when you are more calm and can talk this through. In more dramatic situations, you could send them to their room, and ask them to think of the same thing, and tell them that you will discuss this when you are ready. This gives both of you a "time out" from each other and reduces the risk of saying something either of you might regret.

This technique also improves your child's ability to think. Let's say your child went to someone's house, someone with whom you know he doesn't get along that well. Sure enough he comes home all upset because he's just had yet another fight with this person. In your head you already know that they should have found someone else to play with. As they are mentally "rewinding" the scenario, you may have to guide them to the very beginning of the "video" and help them discover that if he had chosen someone else to play with, all the trouble could have been avoided.

EXERCISE:
The next time your child is upset or in trouble, ask them to "rewind the video" to where the trouble started, and figure out a new ending to the scenario. Write it down here:

_____
_____
_____

EXPECTATIONS

Clear, realistic expectations should always be our goal. Referring to your non-negotiables is a good way to start. Have you been pretty consistent with this, or do you often change your mind, randomly adding or deleting from your list of expectations? Just like adults, children do not like surprises when it comes to your expectations. If your boss said you had a week to complete a task, and then suddenly wants it in a day, I'm sure that would not sit well with you. If, in analyzing your non-negotiables, you find that they are not working out, then tweak them, and let your children know you've altered your expectations of their behavior.

The other aspect of expectations I would like to discuss is setting realistic goals. Just as in reading, children have an "instructional" level and a "frustration" level, so too it is with expectations. Our expectations have to be clear and reasonable, otherwise they become frustrating to our children. I have sat in on meetings when parents say to their children that if they get straight 'A's next card marking, they can get a new puppy. Now that's a double whammy. First of all it's *extrinsically* motivating, meaning they will be driven by wanting a puppy, rather than wanting good grades. Secondly, if this child has been failing or close to failing, how realistic is it to expect that they go from that to straight A's in just 10 weeks? Parents are certainly setting them up for failure. If they go from D's and F's to B's and C's that is considerable progress. Yet in the child's eyes, that is going to be failure, since it wasn't straight A's. They will give up that much sooner since they feel it's hopeless, then you will be right back where you started.

If you are in a situation that requires improvement on your children's part, be it grades, maintaining their room or whatever, once again sit down with them. Discuss what is realistic and acceptable and, together, map a plan to carry it out.

Sound familiar? I hope so, because that strategy works in just about any situation, whether it's related to behavior or achievement. It is these investments of time that will bring you closer to your child, and gain more influence upon them for when you are not there to help them make the sensible choice.

EXERCISE:

Write down 2 or 3 expectations you have of *each child* that relate to behavior and achievement. Try to be as specific and concrete as possible

BEHAVIOR: EXAMPLE: (*bed made before they leave for school, no physical fights with siblings, help make lunches for school*)

Child #1
1. _____
2. _____
3. _____

ACHIEVEMENT: EXAMPLE (homework completed accurately, A's and B's on report cards)
4. _____
5. _____
6. _____

Who Says Kids Don't Come With A Manual?

Child #2 BEHAVIOR:
   1._____
   2._____
   3._____

ACHIEVEMENT
   4._____
   5._____
   6._____

Child #3 BEHAVIOR:
   1._____
   2._____
   3._____

ACHIEVEMENT
   4._____
   5._____
   6._____

Now ask yourself,

1. Is your child clear on these expectations? How do you know?
_____
_____

2. Do you need to either adjust or discuss them with your child? How so?
_____
_____

Louanne Saenz

EXAMPLE

We all know that children learn by example. To a great degree this is true but there are exceptions. I probably shouldn't admit this but, when my boys were younger, and they would play video games, I could hear them swearing when they thought I couldn't hear them. Even though neither I nor my husband swore on a regular basis, they still learned how to swear. When I pointed out that I could hear them, they did apologize. Now I know they swear when they are out with the guys. I am not going to make a huge deal about this. They know, however, that swearing in school or in front of other adults is unacceptable. I'm sure you can think
of other situations where you know a child isn't allowed to do a certain thing in their own home, but out of their parent's sight they try to get away with it. For the most part however, this is more the exception than the rule.

I would like to share a little incident that happened two years ago, when my son was a senior. That was the year I was going through Chemotherapy and radiation. I wanted to make it as normal a year for my family as was humanly possible. I was able to work during my treatments, and cook and pretty much carry on as normal, with an occasional bad day. I really didn't think much of it, although people told me that was pretty amazing. Anyway, my son was captain of his soccer team and they were not having a good season. They weren't just losing by a little, but lost with scores like 9 to 1 or 8 to 3. Still, he hung in there and gave it his all at every game. One day when he came home from yet another game that they had lost miserably, I congratulated him on how he always played his heart out, in spite of their many losses. He turned around and said, "Well look at you, Mom." I said, "What do you mean?" He said, "You have cancer, and you go to chemo, and still work, cook for us, and pretty much do everything you usually

Who Says Kids Don't Come With A Manual?

do. You didn't let anything stop you." I didn't say a word back. I was in too much shock. I had no idea a 17 year old boy even noticed something like that.

I share this story because when you least expect it your children *are* watching you and your reactions to situations, positive and negative. Learning by example is a powerful tool, and should never be underestimated.

Louanne Saenz

"YOU HAVE TO TRY IT. YOU DON'T HAVE TO LIKE IT"

This is a saying I coined in our household for trying new foods. It has worked well in our home. This saying also works well in several other situations. If your child is reluctant to join any type of camp or summer activity, and you're sure he will enjoy something, offer him the two choices you think he will most enjoy. Then tell him that he has to try one of them, at least for this particular summer or whatever season it happens to be. Then if he doesn't like it, he never has to try it again. This eliminates arguing about which activity to join, and gives him an out if he doesn't end up liking it.

Another situation in which this was used was for medication. A child was reluctant to try Ritalin, yet he was failing everything, and getting in considerable trouble at recess. A Learning Disability had been ruled out, and his diagnosis of Attention Deficit Disorder was severe, not just borderline. His parent told him he had to try the medication, at least for one card marking, then if he didn't like it, he had to give a reason as to why he didn't like it, and it couldn't be just "because".

This saying can work in any situation that a child is going to be trying for the first time, be it professional counseling, getting a tutor, or calling a friend he might be nervous about calling. It helps kids take small initial risks, yet feel they will be heard after a trial period.

TALKING TO YOUR CHILDREN
(SUMMARY)

This section is a summary of sections of the manual that have addressed talking to your children in more specific ways.

ATTENTION:

Point out specific positive behaviors as they're happening. *"I really appreciate you remembering to take out the garbage on your own."*

EMOTIONAL INTELLIGENCE:

Ask questions that help them evaluate and show evidence of their behavior and accomplishments. *"Do you think you did better, worse or stayed the same?" "How do you know?"*

EMPATHY:

Put yourself in their place. Include some type of "feeling" word. *"Wow it must be <u>disappointing</u> to lose after working so hard!" "You must really be <u>excited</u> about that 'A'. All that studying sure paid off!"*

ENCOURAGEMENT:

It is specific and non-judgmental. *"Last month it took you 15 minutes to read a page. Now it only takes you 10. That's progress!"*

HOMEWORK:

Sit down when you are both calm. State your concerns, then

together develop a plan. *"I am very worried about this homework issue. We need to make some serious changes. Let's figure out what's getting in the way, then come up with a plan to tackle it."*

MESSAGES:

"Being" Messages: Unearned, more general, *"You are my sunshine."*
"Doing" Messages: Earned, recognition for accomplishment, *"Whoa, you did that all by yourself, Way to go!"*
"I" Messages: *I get _____ when you _____ because _____.*
Please_____.

QUESTIONING:
Ask rather than tell. *Instead of* "You shouldn't have done that, ask *"Do you think it was a good idea to do that"*

NOTE: This technique is tougher to remember and implement. Give yourself time. Once you get the hang of it though, it's with you forever!

REWARDS & PUNISHMENT:
When your child asks you what he's going to get for being good, simply say, *"I will not pay you to be good. That is what you should automatically be doing."*

"REWIND THE VIDEO" Remember this is a strategy to help kids think of how the trouble started, thereby creating a happier ending in which no one gets in trouble.

UNDOING YOUR MISTAKES: *Please get out of here, before I say something I'll regret!"*

Who Says Kids Don't Come With A Manual?

"YOU HAVE TO TRY IT. YOU DON'T HAVE TO LIKE IT." In the section of the same name. This line is used for any first time trials, i.e. food, medication.

Section 4:

DISCIPLINE

- A. Discipline
- B. Consequences
- C. Influence
- D. Motivation
- F. Rewards / Punishment

DISCIPLINE

On the first day of my Adolescent Psychology class, our professor told us a story of how he stood in the middle of a mall one day and randomly asked people "How do you get to the moon?" Of course no one had a clue. Then he asked people, "What's wrong with today's kids?" Of course everyone had an answer to that. His point was that we, in fact, have figured out how to get to the moon, but unfortunately haven't totally figured out the answer to childhood discipline. It often gets confused with punishment. Discipline and punishment though, are two totally different matters. What helped me realize this was looking at the word "discipline." Its root word, disciple, means follower. In other words, we as parents are the teachers and our children are our followers. Hence, discipline's goal should be to *teach* as opposed to punishment's goal, which simply *hurts*.

How do you know if you are using discipline or punishment? Discipline is reasonable and related to whatever it is they did wrong. Punishment is not, and ultimately hurts both you and your child. If your child comes in half an hour past curfew do you ground them for a week or two or adjust their curfew next time they go out? If they are mean to their sibling, again, do you ground them or separate them? In most cases you should be able to think of a related consequence to whatever it is they did wrong. If you are too upset or cannot think of an appropriate disciplinary action immediately, a very effective technique is to send them to their room until you do think of one, or calmly say to them you will discuss this further with dad or another close adult, and then let them know what will be done.

As both a mother and elementary counselor, appropriate discipline is something I've addressed on almost a daily basis. Consider this example. Your child has lied to you about breaking something, and you know for a fact he did it. The goal here is to teach honesty for the future, and not humiliate or shame him for lying. Depending on what it is they broke they would of course need to pay you to replace it. If they don't have the money, they could earn it by completing various chores. When you're both calm, you could have a short talk about why he lied in the first place. If he says he's afraid of getting into trouble, simply agree that, yes, some kind of consequence has to happen, and that the more honest he is the less severe it would need to be.

EXERCISE:

1. Your child has just taken a toy away from his sibling. The sibling comes to tell you about it. You:
   a) Make him give it back
   b) Listen to both sides of the story and decide what to do.
   c) Have them figure out what to do.

2. Your child tells you he has no homework. The next day he brings home a missing assignment slip. You:
   a) Ground him for lying
   b) Have him do the assignment and take whatever other consequence at school.
   C) Make him miss something he was planning on attending (hockey practice, a party).

ANSWERS

1. C. If your children are over four years old, letting them solve the issue takes you out of the role of being judge and jury. You want to avoid this role as much as possible, because any time you have to "rule," you are turning one child against you and the siblings against each other. That is the problem with both A & B. If your children are under four, however, you may want to go with B, and figure out a solution *together*, until they are old enough to figure it out for themselves.

Who Says Kids Don't Come With A Manual?

NOTE: If your children cannot seem to play together without creating a risky situation for themselves, then it's fine to intervene by separating them for a while. This gives equal treatment and if they would rather play with each other, then they will be motivated to learn how to get along better in the future. You may need to discuss how to do that before the next time they play together.

2. **B.** This gets you out of having to deal with it yourself. This situation is ultimately between him and his teacher. Your job is to support the teacher. A, grounding him has nothing to do with the fact that he lied, and C, again is not related to what he did, and will only build further resentment toward you.

Keep in mind that discipline needs to relate back to their misbehavior. To use the cliché, "The punishment has to fit the crime". For example, if time or money is the issue, then they need to pay it back.

CONSEQUENCES

Discipline and consequences go hand-in-hand. One always impacts the other. Ineffective discipline equals ineffective consequences and vice versa. Based largely on the work of Raymond Levy Ph. D., and Jim Fay, I have organized my explanation of consequences around a "menu" from which you can choose what would work best in your particular situations.

Please remember, sometimes the only difference between punishment and consequence is your tone of voice. I know that is easier said than done. That is why I suggest that whenever possible you *delay* delivering the consequence until you've had a chance to calm down. To quote Jim Fay, **"Always deliver a negative content message with a positive relationship message."** For example, *"It breaks my heart to have to do this,* (***positive*** relationship message) *but you leave me no choice. You will not be able to go to the party this weekend since you did not follow curfew last weekend."* (***negative*** content message) "Next week you can try again." This way, the consequence becomes the bad guy, not you.

Please also keep this caveat in mind from Dr. Raymond Levy, **"Rules without relationships equals rebellion".** This manual is all about relationships. If parents want to enforce rules in a consistent manner, they need to have a positive relationship with their children. Having a positive relationship will help children to accept the rules more easily, thus giving parents the best chance of *influencing* their children's actions. Parents, choose your battles carefully. Always return to the non-negotiables you listed in Section One and realize that *everything else* is up for discussion and compromise.

In deciding which consequence to use, ask yourself what you are trying to teach your child. If it is responsibility, as in the case of missing homework, you need to ask yourself what will make them uncomfortable enough to raise their level of concern without humiliating them. For the more impulsive child, or chronic offender, you may have to use impacting consequences more often. Unfortunately, they need the "shock" value to help them remember. For most children however, a milder consequence usually suffices.

A Menu of Consequences
Appetizer
Natural Consequences (They naturally occur)
Example, *they forget their lunch, they go hungry*

Main Course
Logical consequences: Your Choice of

RELATED: Connected to what they have done
Examples: *They break something, they pay for it; they disobey curfew, curfew is shortened or withdrawn altogether (depending on how many times this has already happened); they don't do their homework, they make it up, then do an extra assignment.*

Your turn:
Behavior_____
Related Consequence_____

RELEVANT: Practicing the appropriate or desired behavior
Example: *They call someone a name, they practice writing something nice about them at an **inconvenient** time and then saying those things to him/her*
Your turn:
Behavior_____
Relevant Consequence_____

Louanne Saenz

IMPACTING: Having them do something they really dread, so as to grab their attention. (Warning: this could cause resentment, be sure to serve with positive relationship message).

Example: *Cleaning the bathrooms and inside the refrigerator for skipping chores, taking away driving or phone privileges for skipping homework.*
<u>**Your turn:**</u>
Behavior_____
Impacting Consequence_____

<u>*Dessert*</u>

Delayed Consequence: If you're not sure what to do, tell them you'll get back to them once you've figured out the appropriate consequence.

INFLUENCE

I wish a synonym existed for influence that began with 'A' so that this would be the first section you read in this manual. If there is anything I want you to memorize it is this: ***The amount of influence you have over your child will be directly proportionate to the strength of your relationship.*** Think of people who have influenced you. How strong a relationship do or did you have with them? Were you ever convinced to do something you were otherwise reluctant to do, based on the relationship you had with that person? This could have been a parent, boss or spouse.

Do not confuse influence with influential. There may be people in our lives who are influential that we have never met, but have just heard about. We admire certain qualities in them, which inspire us to greater heights. Just as these people can be inspirational in our lives, so can you as parents have influence, even when you are not around your children. I think that is every parent's dream. Wouldn't it be nice if we could perch ourselves on our children's shoulders, like Jiminy Cricket did with Pinocchio, and be their conscience? The closest thing we will ever have to that is influence.

Again no shortcuts exist to influencing anyone. Just like respect, influence is earned. People who spend time with us, both in fun and during stress will influence us. I return to what Glasser describes as need-satisfying relationships. If your children feel LOVED because of what you say (messages, spoken and unspoken) and do for them, feel a sense of POWER and FREEDOM because of the choices they are allowed to make for themselves, and have FUN with you on a pretty regular basis, you certainly have a much better chance at influencing them.

Rewards and punishments are feeble attempts at shortcuts to influence. They are manipulative because they run the risk of making the reward and punishment more important than the action being encouraged or stifled. Replace rewards with spontaneous celebrations, and punishments with consequences.

EXERCISE:
Ask yourself the following questions about your child. Then ask your child the same things. (If they are reluctant to answer, tell them it's your homework assignment and you need their help!) Try not to get pulled into an argument with them on any of these questions. If they can't think of anything, make a few suggestions yourself (from when you completed the exercise) and see if they agree. They do not need to be asked in any particular order. Start with whatever you think will be easiest for them to answer first.

1. How do they know that they are loved? (LOVE & BELONGING) Ask for specific examples.
   _____
   _____
   ____

2. How are they recognized for accomplishments they achieve? (PERSONAL POWER) Be as specific as possible.
   _____
   _____

3. What choices are they given as children? (FREEDOM)
   _____

4. What FUN do you have together on a regular basis? _____

Who Says Kids Don't Come With A Manual?

Based on their answers, come up with an influence factor from 1 (No influence) to 10 (Most influence)

_____

MOTIVATION

Of all the topics presented in this manual, motivation is probably the most difficult to explain and totally comprehend, because of its complexity. I'd like to blame Pavlov for part of this problem. Remember him? He was the Russian physiologist who studied motivation using dogs. In his experiments, he presented food in connection with the sound of a bell. At the sight of food, dogs naturally salivated. After a few trials, he then rang the bell without bringing out food, and the dogs still salivated. His conclusion was that dogs could be conditioned to respond to a certain stimuli (motivators). From that conclusion, the behaviorist movement was born. People were substituted for animals. Since then, man has attempted to condition (motivate) man to respond to just about any stimuli.

This is especially true about children. Adults use tempting motivators on children in the form of rewards and punishments. These are dangled over their heads in an effort to **externally motivate** (condition) them. If any of you have done this, you know it usually doesn't work. If it does work, it is temporary, and the stakes continually need to be raised. Numerous studies have been conducted on people of all ages. In these studies, two groups are assigned identical tasks. One group is told they would be rewarded, while the other group is told nothing. Invariably the group **not** rewarded out-performed the group given a reward. It was observed that the **rewarded** group took shortcuts in an effort to get their prize as soon as possible. In other words the reward became more important than the task at hand. This is the problem with external motivation.

To make a task **intrinsically motivating**, I return to William Glasser's work. He states that in order to make something intrinsically motivating, it needs to be a need-satisfying experience. Children need to derive some type of satisfaction through any or all of their basic needs, be it fun, a sense of accomplishment (power), of love and belonging, or a feeling of choice in the matter (freedom). This is not always easy. Here are some guidelines to begin accomplishing this.

1. If you are going to use external motivation, it should be for simple tasks. For example if they remember to brush their teeth all week, they can stay up later on the weekend.
2. Try to have the reward be a privilege rather than something tangible.
3. The more complex the task, steer away from external motivation.
4. To make an experience intrinsically rewarding (motivating), sit down with your child and discuss the obstacles at hand. Be open-minded, otherwise your child will consider this a waste of time. Develop a plan and a time period within which you will implement the plan without changes. Refer to the Homework (section 6) or Chores (section 5) as a plan you might use.
5. Adjust the plan if necessary, *after* the initial trial period that was agreed upon. If the plan has gone particularly well, celebrate! It could be a trip to the video store, being allowed to stay up late, or having a friend spend the night. The difference here is that the celebration is spontaneous, not planned, as it would have been in an externally motivating situation.
6. There are no shortcuts! If improvement in behavior or achievement is the goal, then the experience needs to become need satisfying.
7. Consider this an investment of your time and not an expense. If you don't invest the time up front, you will only spend it in yelling, nagging or some other type of negative interaction.

Motivating ourselves is a component of emotional intelligence. In studies on motivation it also has been said that we can't expect people to be intrinsically motivated in everything. Some possess a stronger drive to succeed than others. Finding the right leverage and balance will take time.

For me, exercising was simply not an intrinsically motivating experience. I always knew that I should exercise on a regular basis, and envied the people that could wake up early and do just that. Finally I discovered a video that I could follow in my own home. For the first time in my life I am exercising on a regular basis, even though I still don't do it at the crack of dawn! My point simply is that you have to know what you are willing to do or not do, to reach a goal, and guide your children in doing the same. Just as I knew I needed to exercise, children know what they need to do. Creating the atmosphere in which to do this can be a challenge. Listen to your children and know what they can and cannot handle in order to motivate them toward their goals.

Some parents claim their children really don't care about anything, and would rather fail than try. This type of passive-aggressive behavior could require professional counseling. Also if it is a school-related issue, check with your child's teacher to determine if the child *can't* do the work or *won't* do it.

A final editorial I would like to make about this topic is on the parental expectation of just how much "fun" school should be, as a way of motivating children. I have attended numerous meetings in which a parent has no problem with his child hurting himself, risking serious injury, and tolerating a coach's often harsh remarks, all in the name of mastering a sport. Yet the moment a subject becomes the least bit challenging, parents are complaining that expectations are unrealistic, and that school isn't fun. I share this observation in an effort to once again ask yourself how consistent are you in the amount of struggling you expect your children to encounter, and the amount of support you are willing to offer toward motivating them to succeed?

Who Says Kids Don't Come With A Manual?

EXERCISE:

Think of a situation(s) in your household that you have tried to handle with *external* motivation. (rewards or punishment) EXAMPLE: *Giving money for every "A" on their report card.*

SITUATION #1

_____
_____
_____

SITUATION #2

_____
_____
_____

SITUATION #3

_____
_____
_____

Now think of how you can make that situation more *intrinsically* motivating.

EXAMPLE: *I will spend more time helping them with their more challenging homework. If too many battles occur, I will share the task with my spouse, other siblings that are willing to help, or find an outside tutor.*

SITUATION #1

_____
_____
_____

Louanne Saenz

SITUATION #2

SITUATION #3

REWARDS / PUNISHMENT

This topic has been addressed in the section on "Motivation." At this point I simply want to again reiterate the disadvantages of, what author Alfie Kohn describes as, "different sides of the same coin." This means that **both** reward and punishment are *externally* motivating tactics. With rewards, the stakes get higher each time, and becomes more important than the task. Likewise with punishment, if a child does something wrong, they are more upset over the punishment, rather than experiencing remorse for what they have done wrong.

Several years ago I attended a workshop held by Dr. Joyce Brothers. She was also talking about punishment and proceeded to tell about an experiment with mice. The mice were trained to press a button in order to get their food. After a period of time, they wanted to un-train the mice. When one group of mice pressed the button nothing happened any longer. They pressed it a few more times and nothing happened still. That was the end of it and they learned quite quickly that pressing the button no longer lead to food.

The other group of mice, however, was given an electric shock when they pressed the button. These mice would then cower, go to the corner and lie still. After a long time, they would try again and, of course, the same thing happened. Each time they were shocked, it would take them much longer to try pressing the button again. In other words, the "punished" mice took considerably longer to learn that food would no longer come after pressing the button. The point of the experiment was to help realize that children do not "learn their lesson" faster when punished.

In keeping with my "replace not erase" motto, (section 1E) then I suggest you replace punishment with discipline (consequences) and rewards with celebrations. Discipline, as you recall, **teaches** rather than hurts. Consequences are often the tools of discipline. Consequences, as often as possible, should be related to what they have done. (section 4B) Be careful though. Sometimes the only difference between a consequence and punishment is your tone of voice. If you are still ranting and raving to your child that you are going to "teach them a lesson, once and for all!" what you're really implying is "I'm going to punish you so bad you won't ever forget this."

So remember to try and deliver the consequence once you've had a chance to calm down.

Please don't agonize over this however. If you do yell and scream and later regret it, that's progress, too. Remember you can only *reduce* the times you will yell and scream, not *eliminate* them. Another option you have is to admit to your child that you gave too harsh a consequence, because you were so upset at the time. Maybe you grounded him for two weeks, when in reality one weekend would have been enough. (Remember grounding is appropriate if what they did wrong had something to do with disobeying you while they were out somewhere). It is acceptable to say that you were very upset when you gave that consequence, and that one weekend of grounding will be sufficient. Chances are he will be ecstatic and you've once again enhanced your relationship with him. It also sets the example of admitting a mistake, a trait we certainly want to develop in our children as well. Just be advised not to do this too often. They might begin to think that you will do this all the time, and consequently not take you seriously.

Rewards have a similar effect as punishment. At my school, many students are put on a daily note plan for work and/or behavior. In spite of my parent warnings to steer away from reward, the students tell me all about the new puppy or video they are going to get if they get positive notes. Invariably the notes do start out pretty positive. This success lasts a week or so until the first negative note comes home. Then the student gets furious over what he is not going to get, gets mad at his parents, and the teacher feels caught in the middle. It is far more effective to discuss their negative behavior, and what they could do instead in the future, followed by some type of consequence for repeated negative notes. Similarly when a positive note comes home, discuss that, and spontaneously celebrate if they have had a particularly good week. The child enjoys the surprise, and the success will breed further success.

Remember, any attempt to change behavior, will inevitably result in occasional bad days. Once again, a discussion utilizing the "rewind the video" technique (section 3K) to where the trouble started with a plan of what to do differently for the future can be most helpful. If they encounter two or three consecutive bad days, it is fine to give a consequence. Removal of a privilege is one suggestion. It is also appropriate, but not absolutely necessary to say at the onset of the plan that if they do have a few bad days, something will need to happen at home to help them improve their behavior at school. This can take many forms. If the child has been mean to another child, they could write a note of apology. If they misbehaved at recess, they may have some type of "recess" time at home be reduced or eliminated for a period of time.

This is where a little creativity goes a long way. Sometimes *reducing* the amount of play time, rather than eliminating it altogether can be more impacting. For example, your policy is that your child plays after homework is completed, and only until a certain time. They abuse this by coming home late. Next time, you reduce their outside play to 15 minutes. Just as he starts to have fun, it becomes time to stop. This consequence can be more impacting than not going out at all. I use this technique at school. If students chronically have missing assignments, then they make them up at recess. If they complete them before recess is over, then they can go out.

Louanne Saenz

Many times, it ends up being only five minutes. Just as they start to have fun it's time to come in. They don't like it, and often they remember that feeling for next time. Again you may refer to the Consequence section (4B).

EXERCISE:

Think of how you can replace some type of *reward* you typically give with a *celebration*.
_____
_____

Now think of how you can replace a typical *punishment* with natural or logical *consequence*.
_____
_____

Section 5:

HOME SURVIVAL

- A. Allowances
- B. Allergies / Antibiotics
- C. Bedtime
- D. Chores
- E. Kitchen Capers

ALLOWANCES

Two questions parents often have about allowances are, 1) "Should allowances be earned or automatically given?" 2) "How much is appropriate?" In order to answer the first question, ask yourself this question. What is my purpose in giving allowance? If your purpose in giving allowance is to help your child manage their own money, then you probably feel it should be automatically given. If your purpose is to pay them for chores around the house, then you believe it should be earned.

Now consider the message you are sending with the first response. Money is something you will need to manage in life, so here is a little to practice with. In the second response, the message implied is, "Everything in life has a price tag, and this is what doing your chores is worth."

Most of the research will agree more with the first response. Surprised? The flaw in the second way of thinking is that if every chore has a price tag, then children do nothing as a way of helping, simply because it's the right thing to do. The real purpose of allowances is to help children manage money. Kids need to have a set of chores expected of them as a way of doing their fair share. However if there are some tasks around the house that are over and above the usual expectations, then there is no harm in paying children to do those, especially if they want to earn some extra money.

It may be hard to digest giving children allowances for the sake of it. The thinking trap here is well if they don't do their chores, then they're not getting any allowance. Withdrawing allowance for not doing chores is most likely ineffective. For now, trust the fact that allowances are more for money management than anything else.

What about the second question, "How much is appropriate?" Many factors play into this especially your own

Louanne Saenz

family budget. A rule of thumb you may want to consider is a dollar per grade or age, depending on what you can afford. Varying the amounts based on age or grade is easily understood by kids, and teaches that fair is not always equal. Explaining this logic to your children is also a good relationship builder.

ALLERGIES / ANTIBIOTICS

While my intention is not to dispense medical advice, since I am not a physician, I do want to share with you some interesting research I have discovered pertaining to these two subjects. In the vast majority of cases of A.D.D. in our building, parents mentioned their child had been on antibiotics, for repeated ear infections (Otitis Media). When I looked into this further I discovered two things.

First, repeated ear infections are most often caused by allergies to milk, gluten and wheat. We all know how much milk and wheat are a significant part of most children's diet. Gluten is a type of yeast, and is in just about everything that contains wheat. If your child suffers from chronic ear infections, you may want to ask your physician about this.

The second, more disturbing fact I discovered is the effect that repeated use of antibiotics is suspected to have on a child's nervous system. Simply stated, repeated use of antibiotics sets up an unhealthy cycle, destroying both friendly and unfriendly bacteria in the digestive tract. Antibiotics however, do not effect candida yeasts in the digestive tract. Consequently, yeast overgrowth occurs, upsetting the balance in the body. This causes what has been called a "leaky gut." As a result, more food allergens and toxins get absorbed, producing various symptoms. These can include, among others fatigue, headache, depressions and hyperactivity.

Investigators found that 69% of the hyperactive children they studied gave a history of greater than 10 ear infections. I share these findings with you, so that if your child does suffer from repeated ear infections or any repeated infection requiring the use of antibiotics, you may look into alternatives. Incidentally it was also noted that sugar promotes yeast growth as well.

I was disappointed to find out that many physicians are not

Louanne Saenz

aware of this research. With A.D.D. only getting more and more common, we need to both become aware and make those in the medical community aware of this research in order to possibly reduce its occurrence.

BEDTIME

Bedtime can be smooth or stressful, depending on several factors. Do you have children that simply don't want to go to bed, afraid they will miss something good, stalling by asking for countless drinks of water or just one more story? Bedtime can prove challenging to even the most patient of parents. Let's begin by breaking bedtime into a few different problem areas.

GETTING READY FOR BED: Do your kids have a set time, a set ROUTINE such as bath, brush teeth, and in bed for a story? Just as mornings go smoother if a routine is in place, so too will bedtime. Get their input on what an appropriate routine is. The chances of them following it are far greater if they have had some say in how it will go. It's often helpful for young children who don't tell time yet, to say to them that after a certain show is over, they know it's time for bed. Some children need that mental preparation to begin winding down.

Do you have persistent bedtime STALLERS in your home? Some firm yet gentle coaxing can work great. Again if a routine is firmly established, however this should remedy any excuses to delay going to bed. If after bath, a drink and or snack and final bedtime story, they still are stalling, one final suggestion would be to leave them in their room for quiet time, say 10 minutes, followed by lights out. Period.

STAGGERING BEDTIMES can work wonders. Just staggering their bedtimes ten minutes apart so that individual time is spent with each child can go very far in building relationships. The oldest child particularly likes this idea since they get to go to bed later of course. Typically oldest kids feel cheated because they are often blamed for arguments, since they are the oldest and should know better. They probably also have more chores than their siblings. Letting them stay up later can make up for some of these other disadvantages. In the Attention section (7), it is noted that 20 minutes of one-on-one time was found to reduce whining and aggressive behavior. Reading a favorite book or talking about your day together can certainly fulfill at least 10 of that 20 minute time. If children share a room, staggering can be more difficult but not impossible. If they each know they are getting that individual time with you, at least on some nights, they should agree to it.

One other situation I'd like to discuss is when **children wake up in the middle of the night to sleep with you**. I am amazed by how many parents admit that their kids sleep with them on a regular basis. Here's a suggestion that worked great in our family. I had read this idea and tried it with our daughter. Before she went to bed, I told her that we made her a "special bed" on the floor next to our bed. We used a sleeping bag with a favorite sheet and a pillow. She was told that was where she would sleep if she woke up in the middle of the night. It worked beautifully. It lasted only a few nights, and then she stayed in her own room after that.

If kids do wake up, this happens typically around age three or so because that is when they develop fears. Remember fears are learned and fear of the dark is common. Using the "special bed" approach is a nice compromise and sends the gentle message that everyone sleeps in his or her own bed.

When my boys were younger, they preferred to sleep together in one room, and turned the other bedroom into a separate playroom. They are only 13 months apart so this worked well. Getting creative with various bedtime setups can be fun and teach your children once again, the value of compromise and negotiation.

CHORES

Chores are easily one of the major sources of conflict for parents and children. On the flip side, it can also be one of those great teachable moments to model negotiation and compromise, two important life skills to have. Whenever this topic arose in parenting classes, it was difficult to talk about anything else because of their exasperation over this subject. On the one hand parents are giving their children a litany of chores to complete, while children are thinking, "I have way better things to do than this", or "who cares if you can't see the floor in my room." I wish I had a magic bullet for this dilemma. What I can offer are some ideas to and consider when the topic of chores does arise.

Beginning around First grade, you may want to start with one chore. For example, they make their bed daily. You could begin to teach them some other weekly task such as setting or clearing the table. As with allowance, you may also want to use the same general guideline with chores, the number of chores corresponds to their grade level. By fourth grade then, they could be making their bed, sorting, folding or putting away laundry, setting or clearing the table, loading or emptying the dishwasher. Sound good? It can happen. Please do keep this in mind. Kids do NOT automatically know how to do these things. It can also take a while for them to do these things independently, and without reminders. You have probably also discovered that everyone would rather do one type and no one wants to do another type. Again compromise, by taking turns.

As children get older and busier, again you may find you need to assign fewer but perhaps more time consuming chores. Establish a day and time frame as to when you expect it to be done, then, get a more exact time from them (within the half hour) as to what time they will complete it. I used to phrase the time (not the chore) as a choice. For example, I would ask, "Do you want to vacuum at 10 or 11:00? They agree to do it at 11:00, **then I write this down in a visible place** such as a magnetic board on the fridge or cork board in their room. I also used to set the oven timer, so that when it buzzed I could remind them of their agreement. Then a gentle reminder at 11:00 that that was the time they agreed upon is all they needed. My husband was always amazed at how well this technique worked. I don't mean to imply that chores were never an issue in our home. This method did increase their chance of completing chores more often.

At this point, I have to briefly comment about the Number 1 complaint about kids: their messy, often smelly rooms. Once again here are a few suggestions:

1. If they are young (under 10) offer to do it with them at a mutually acceptable time. You will be surprised how quickly it gets done.
2. Make a specific list of what you expect done, i.e. dirty clothes in hamper, toys in boxes, bed made, no food or dirty dishes. Post the list.
3. Explain the difference between straightening (putting things away, making the bed) and cleaning (dusting and vacuuming).
4. Have them play music as they clean.
5. Decide on a particular day of the week that it gets done. Then ease up a bit the rest of the week.
6. Invest in some good storage materials for their rooms. This can make a huge difference.
7. Shut their door!

EXERCISE:
Before you actually discuss the subject of chores, make a list of what you would like them to do. Estimate how long it should take.

Who Says Kids Don't Come With A Manual?

1. _____ time it takes _____
2. _____ time it takes _____
3. _____ time it takes _____
4. _____ time it takes _____
5. _____ time it takes _____
6. _____ time it takes _____

Once you've done this, then approach them and be open to discussion and compromise. You may think about rotating the unpopular chores or offering to do it yourself in return for something else.

I know parents really get frustrated on this topic, me included. If you think back to the exercise on behavior (section 2) however, and know that they do have other responsible habits, it may offer some comfort. That is how I survived the messy room dilemma. This got to be more of a problem as teenagers, when their lives got really hectic. Sometimes, if I had the time, I would go in and straighten their room and it would take me 15 to 30 minutes. I'd find myself asking, "Do I really want to ruin a relationship over half an hour or over an unmade bed?" For me the answer is unquestionably "No"!

KITCHEN CAPERS

Since so much of family life centers around the kitchen and mealtimes, I wanted to spend some time on that topic. Firstly, how often do you as a family have meals together? Hopefully it's at least four or five times a week, when they're young. In studies done on achievement, the common factor discovered was the fact that families spent mealtimes together. As children do get older and busier, it does become more difficult to accomplish this. Whenever possible do make the effort to spend meals together. It's a bonding experience and strengthens the influence you will have on your children.

Many chores center on the kitchen as well. These would include setting and clearing the table, loading and unloading the dishwasher, helping prepare meals, and so on. In our house we typically assigned these chores on a weekly, rotating basis, for simplicity's sake. If we knew someone was going to run late or have to leave early for dinner, then the kids learned to work around this by trading chores that day. Some kids prefer to cook or do particular kitchen chores. This is a great opportunity to have that child perhaps do more in the kitchen in return for less in some other chore.

For the child who was going to miss out on the regular mealtime, I found it easier to make up a plate for them that they could simply microwave, rather than them getting out the leftovers and cleaning up after themselves. It saved a lot of arguing over the quality of how they put everything back in place.

What about the picky eater? I've seen both extremes where parents either ALWAYS or NEVER accommodate their kids. Let's strive for somewhere in between. We all know that as children there were certain foods we did not care for, but then grew up to enjoy them. If that's the case, making something different for the kids and for the adults could be an option. If only one person doesn't like a particular meal, then I made sure there was always something around they could make for themselves. Food was something I didn't want to battle, because of the eventual risk of eating disorders. As long as they ate most of what was on their plate, and didn't waste a lot, we left it at that.

We had a saying in our home, "You have to try it. You don't have to like it." Whenever I prepared something new, everyone had to at least try it. Then they could decide if they liked it or not. In most cases, they usually liked it, and it reduced many battles over food.

What if you do have someone that seems to be pickier than normal. Check out their other sensory reactions. Do they not eat lunch because they can't stand the SMELL when they open the container, or only like certain textures of food? Do they go crazy if a sock is slightly damp or if they FEEL the tag in the back of their clothes? Do they over or under-react to loud SOUNDS? If your child is experiencing other sensory issues, they may have what is called sensory-motor dysfunction. This is a relatively new field. A good occupational therapist is trained in dealing with this. You may want to check this out with through child's pediatrician.

Louanne Saenz

EXERCISE:

List some common kitchen chores that can be rotated on a weekly basis.

1. _____
2. _____
3. _____
4. _____
5. _____
6. _____

Section 6:

SCHOOL SURVIVAL

    A. Homework
    B. Literacy
    C. "What Can I Do at Home?"
    D. Extracurricular Activities

HOMEWORK

Being an educator and parent for over 20 years, homework is probably something on which I could write a whole other book. I will attempt to summarize my suggestions on this subject for you.

As I stated before, in our household the two non-negotiables were school and church. Part of school obviously is homework, so therefore it was a non-negotiable as well. My children knew I would never write a note excusing them from homework. If they ever tried to tell me they were too busy, then an after school activity was forfeited, rather than homework. I have sat through countless meetings with parents who claim their children try to get out of doing homework. In a vast majority of these situations however, I always detected that homework wasn't necessarily a priority. How did I know this? Because whatever suggestion we made, they had an excuse not to do it.

If you truly want to conquer a homework dilemma, here are some suggestions. This will require a serious commitment on your part, for change to really take place. Careful planning will be critical. I can tell you that I have done just about every one of these ideas, and they work. By the way, the younger your child, the easier it will be to enforce this. If you have a middle or high school child, it's going to be harder, and will require some calm discussion that routines need to change. This must be stated with conviction, or your children will once again argue about this. Remember for change to take place, it needs to begin with you!

1. Homework needs to be done first. Do NOT let your child go out and play or watch TV. You will only argue with them to come in, and set yourself up for a negative attitude. A snack followed by a brief planning of homework may be necessary. Assure them they can

play AFTER homework is complete.
2. Establish a specific time for homework. It doesn't have to be the same every day, but the same on Monday, Tuesday etc, depending on activities of everyone involved. Write it down, and post it.
3. Find out from their teacher or other parents what the average amount of time is they are spending on homework. If your child takes considerably longer, then investigate this further. It could be the sign of a learning disability or attention problem.
4. If your child seems overwhelmed by the amount of homework, try this activity. With your help have them ESTIMATE, and write down how long they think each subject will take them to complete. Once complete have them write down the ACTUAL time it took. This simple activity helps keep them focused too, since they're working toward that goal time.
5. Establish a specific place. Some do better near you rather than up in their room where they can daydream.
6. Once you determine that place, have a drawer filled with necessary supplies close by, so that they can't stall looking for these items. Have them tell you when they are running low on something, by writing it on a magnetic board or magnetic tablet posted in a convenient spot for you to see.
7. Determine independent homework from work requiring assistance. If you are unable to help with a particular subject, find someone who can, be it a spouse, older sibling, high school student, neighbor or tutor.
8. If your child's school does not provide one, then invest in a homework planner. There are many cool ones nowadays, that children don't mind filling out. Be sure they have a friend or two's phone number in it that they can call, if they're not sure about something.

9. If they forget a book that's needed then, either take them back to school or get the book from a friend. Have them repay you the time spent getting it, in whatever chore it was you couldn't finish, because of this interruption (related consequence). If forgetting books is a chronic problem, then see if the school has an extra set of books you can check out for home use.
10. Invest in a lapdesk so your child can do homework in the car or at a sibling's practice site if they need to go with you.
11. If you are not sure about what they are telling you is homework, you have two options. 1.) Call a friend to double check the accuracy of what they are telling you. They will usually stop you if they are purposely leaving something out. 2.) If your school has this, check his teacher's webpage for homework updates. If they don't, try emailing the teacher. This should be a last resort however, since this is your child's responsibility, not yours. For some however, it may require this method as a stepping stone to eventually writing down homework more accurately.
12. If your child needs you to take them to the library or pick up something for school, be sure they give you fair warning. This was a huge pet peeve of mine, because children need to understand that we are all busy, and it's only fair they respect that as well.
13. Once homework is complete, you can review it, but it's not absolutely necessary for everything. If you find mistakes, don't point them out. Simply tell them how many mistakes you see, and have them find them. They learn much better by this "discovery" method, and gain independence sooner.
14. Determine the number of appropriate extra-curricular activities you and your child can handle. Some kids can

honestly handle quite a bit, and thrive on it, while others will get stressed if spread too thin.
15. If you think homework is sloppy and they don't, have them deal with their teacher at school about it.

EXCEPTIONAL SITUATIONS:

LATCH KEY:

If your child must attend latch key, see if they can designate a spot to complete at least some of their homework there. If they are older and home alone, call them at a regular time each day to make sure they have begun.

DIVORCE SITUATIONS:

Homework is often a point of contention between divorced parents. Unfortunately it is the child who suffers in these situations. Here are a couple of suggestions:

Make sure a plan is in place for transferring homework to and from each parent's home. Many a homework sheet is lost between homes, ending up in more fights and frustration.
If one parent is more diligent about completing homework, then that is who should oversee it. This happens even in two parent homes. Try to complete as much as possible with that parent, leaving simpler homework for the other parent. Whenever possible, both parents should attend conferences either together or separately if necessary. Sometimes the other parent doesn't know how to help them and needs some guidance.

EXERCISE:

Select and circle at least five strategies you are willing to implement. Then sit down with your child at a mutually agreed upon time to discuss your concerns, and make clear that this is going to require change on BOTH of your parts. Together come up with a plan, with related consequences for lack of completion. Then at the end of the trial time, evaluate how it went and make any necessary adjustments, again evaluating the plan periodically. Good luck. If you are sincerely determined about conquering the homework war this will definitely improve matters. Don't expect to see improvement overnight. Chances are they have been doing this for a few years, so it may take at least a card marking to get noticeable results.

CONCLUSION:

If you have truly given this your best effort, to no avail, then testing may be the next step. Chances are it could be evidence of a Learning Disability or Attention Deficit Disorder. Both of those terms can make parents cringe. Sit down with your school personnel and be open-minded. Being in denial or placing blame will only result in your child suffering even more. If testing for either a learning disability or A.D.D. is recommended, agree to it. At the very least it can rule something in or out, and you will be that much closer to learning more about how your child thinks, operates, and survives.

Louanne Saenz

LITERACY

Literacy is a topic close to my heart. Being an educator for almost thirty years I have learned some interesting things about this subject. First of all did you know that close to 80% of prisoners are illiterate? While we are spending our taxpayer dollars on expanding prisons, we really need to look at the symptoms in order to do some critical prevention work. When children discover early on that they are not good readers, most often one of two things occurs. They either try to go into hiding, so that no one will notice that they can't read or they become hostile and aggressive. Very often the bullies at school are the struggling readers.

Another observation I would like to point out is that while people are comfortable admitting they can't do Math, or can't draw, or sing, people will rarely ever admit they can't read. If they do admit it, it is very often in a shameful, embarrassing way. That is because people associate being unable to read with being stupid. Even though there are some very famous people who were struggling readers, Einstein and Rockefeller for example, people still think of themselves as stupid if they can't read well.

Regardless of what occupation we choose, reading will be a necessity. We are constantly bombarded with having to read. Now, more than ever with the internet and all its capabilities, being unable to read puts one at a serious disadvantage. Yet the literacy rate is declining rather than rising. This is one area that schools simply cannot do alone. The saying, "It takes a village to raise a child," is most appropriate here.

Schools have come a long ways in the teaching of reading. We have finally struck a nice balance between the teaching of Phonics and Comprehension, the two major components of Reading. Through more sophisticated technology, the medical field is also getting closer and closer to better understanding

Who Says Kids Don't Come With A Manual?

what goes on in the brains of better readers. It still requires additional practice at home however, especially for the child who struggles.

What I have sadly observed is that parents have no problem watching their child struggle at a sports practice, seeing them fall and take hits for example. What I don't understand then is why they expect reading and writing to occur without some kind of struggle as well. Blame is immediately placed on the school, and instead of working together to solve the issue, it becomes a battle. While most children will learn to read regardless of the method used, there will always be that 20% or so that needs a more unique approach to learning to read.

Be HONEST with yourself and your kids about their ability to read. Again in the name of love, parents will tell their child they're doing just fine, when the simple fact is they're not! I know it's difficult to have to communicate to your child that they may not be the best reader. I go back to Jim Fay's advice to deliver a negative content message with a positive relationship message. In this case, you could say to your child that everyone struggles with something. Maybe another sibling struggles with weight, or Math for instance. He or she however struggles with Reading. It doesn't mean they're stupid, it simply means they are going to have to work harder at that particular skill.

Parents often say they don't want their kids to struggle. While this is a perfectly reasonable expectation, it may not be totally realistic, because we know as adults we ALL struggle with something. If you struggled with reading as a child, by all means let them know! They find great comfort in that fact! If you didn't struggle then this is a perfect opportunity for empathy. Share with them how frustrating it must be to have to struggle and stress to them that they will have your unconditional support in this matter. Please don't expect them to overcome it alone or offer bribes if they improve.

Louanne Saenz

As an educator I can offer you some practical tips on helping your child. Keep in mind these three words, TO, WITH & BY, from Margaret Mooney's book *Reading To, With and By Children*.

Parents need to read TO their children. When reading to your child, it can and should be ABOVE their reading level. This is an opportunity to teach comprehension. As you read, check their level of understanding. Use the Who, what, when where and why questions. Depending on their age include "Right There" questions, whose answers are stated right in the text, "Think & Search" which requires a little more "reading between the lines", and for older children (3rd grade and up), "Beyond Text" questions which require drawing conclusions or making inferences. Don't wait until you get to the end of the chapter to ask questions, but at the end of each page, or even after a paragraph. Begin easy so your child experiences success. Gradually sneak in the tougher "Think & Search" and "Beyond Text" questions as they improve.

Parents also need to read WITH their kids. This means taking turns reading together. This should be AT their reading level. Most books indicate the level on the back cover. Make sure you know your child's reading level. Don't assume that if they're in third grade, they are reading at that level. Check with their teacher to make sure. Otherwise it will become a frustrating rather than bonding experience. You can also use the "5 finger rule". Have your child read a page. Every time they make a mistake, put down a finger. If they have made more than 5 mistakes, then it is too hard.

Finally children need to read BY themselves. This of course should be done at their independent reading level. Listen to them read one page. They should not make more than one, sometimes two, mistakes a page. Otherwise they will lose the meaning.

If you are doing some of this at bedtime, a slight variation would be to read TO or WITH your child for 10 to 15 minutes, then leave them to finish reading BY themselves. Doing this three to five nights a week, improves and encourages their love of reading while strengthening your relationship with them. Reading to my children will always be some of my happiest memories with them.

Books are also a very effective way to help your children talk about uncomfortable subjects. If these topics are first presented in a book, whether in fantasy or reality, the chances of them transferring that to their own lives, and talking to you about it are much greater. We see talk on television about the "anti-drug". As far as I'm concerned, books and reading are one of the greatest anti-drugs!

EXERCISE:

Review yours and your family's daily schedule. Based on that, determine at least 4 times during the week that you can consistently read either TO or WITH your child for around 15 minutes. Write those times down:

Day: _____ Time: _____
Day: _____ Time: _____
Day: _____ Time: _____
Day: _____ Time: _____

If you are thinking 4 times is too much, you need to ask yourself, what your true priorities are. Whether your child is struggling or not, reading at home with your child is critical at least through 5th grade.

Louanne Saenz

"WHAT CAN I DO AT HOME?"

This is the question parents most often ask in trying to help their children with school issues. Included in this section, will be a breakdown by subject, with some suggestions as to how you can assist your child at home.

READING/LITERACY:

The section above on Literacy is a good place to start. The "To, With and By" methods explained there are very effective ways of helping your child with reading concerns, particularly at the elementary levels.

If your child is 5 or 6 years old, rhyming games are fun and help develop phonemic awareness, a readiness skill needed for Reading. Other important skills needed are being able to BLEND sounds together and separate or SEGMENT sounds heard in words. You can play this game in the car by taking a simple 2 or 3 sound word and separating each sound or phoneme. For example for "it" you would say 'i' then 't' and have them guess the word. Then work your way to 3, then 4 SOUND (not syllable) words. The flip side of that game would be to say a 2 or 3 sound word and have THEM tell you the individual *sounds*, not letters in the word. If you want to see children really focus and concentrate, try those two exercises. It may even make you think a little! For years we have stressed learning the names of the letters of the alphabet. Research is showing that knowing the sounds in a word are just as, if not more important than, recognizing letter names.

WRITING:

Again if your child is around kindergarten or first grade, a good method to help them write is called scaffolded writing

Who Says Kids Don't Come With A Manual?

based on the approach used in the book, *Scaffolding Emergent Literacy*. If they want to write a sentence like "I went to the park," you would write lines for each word, ideally using a highlighter. Then they write the words on those lines. This helps with spacing, concentration. Notice the lines correspond to the length of the word. At this young age, don't get hung up on accurate spelling. When they are done writing, you can take one or two of the words, and show them the correct spelling. Try to choose the words they spelled almost right, or the shorter, easier words. Do look for letter sound connections though. For example if they spell boat, bot, you know they hear all the sounds. If on the other hand they spell boat tu (I have seen this!) then that needs to be discussed with their teacher. Chances are they are seeing the same thing at school, and this could indicate some learning disabilities.

As children get older, writing will be something they will most likely need at least some assistance. I'm referring to the CONTENT of their writing not, handwriting. Written expression is the category children most often qualify for help, because of the complex process involved. Writing is open-ended, and requires extended concentration, and children need to develop that self-discipline with your help. If they are having trouble, getting started, help them get their thoughts organized. Break up the task into tiny steps. You could help them with the first sentence, tell them you want to see a SPECIFIC number of sentences completed in say, ten minutes, then check on them after that time. As they grow and mature, you should be able to extend both the time and amount they can write independently.

Unfortunately, some children need help with both content and handwriting. Children often struggle with the fine motor control required for writing for many different reasons. Occupational therapy or medication can often improve this situation. While some parents downplay poor handwriting, the simple fact is, writing is required on many standardized state tests. Sure eventually they may have their own secretary or learn to keyboard. They will still need to master basic writing.

SPELLING:

Helping children with spelling, particularly studying for spelling tests has hardly changed over the past 30 years. The standard practice is that students write their misspelled words so many numbers of times. Let me offer you a new way to help your child. Have you or your child fold a standard 8 ½ x11 sheet of paper into 32 squares, or on a computer, insert a table with one inch squares on the entire sheet.

When your child brings their pretest home, instead of seeing if the words are simply right or wrong, add a new category, *logical*. For example if they spell the word least, as 'leest', that is logical as opposed to leet (wrong) which omits the 's' sound altogether. Then using a square for each SOUND not letter, have them re-write it correctly. 'Least' would be written as 'l'-'ea'-'s'-'t' in each square. Then have them highlight the *correct* spelling of the *part* of the word they missed, 'l'-'ea'-'s'-'t'. They can now focus on the part of the word they got wrong. This is a much more concrete and focused way of approaching spelling. Watch their spelling scores soar!

MATH:

If Math is the problem, do activities that are fun for your child. In many school districts, considerably more time is spent on problem solving than on memorizing basic facts. This means that more practice must be spent at home on memorizing basic facts, since mastering them is still required.

Use playing cards and dice to learn addition, subtraction, multiplication and division. Flashcards are the most common way parents use, but for the child who struggles with memorizing, you may have to get more creative. Tape-recording the Math facts, and having the child LISTEN rather than VISUALIZE, may be more helpful for the child who learns better by hearing rather than seeing. Some children do enjoy the old-fashioned workbooks with drill and practice. Be careful with timed exercises. Some children thrive on being timed, while others buckle under that pressure. There are many computer Math games available as well. Your child's teacher will most likely be able to assist you on the better programs that exist.

Sylvia Rymm, author of *Underachievement Syndrome*, suggests the following method for Math homework: Complete the first problem with your assistance, the second problem on their own with you watching for errors, then the rest of the assignment independently. This is another example of small steps taken in order to accomplish the task.

Louanne Saenz

EXTRACURRICULAR ACTIVITIES

I briefly touched on this subject in the Homework section. I just want to point out again the importance of not spreading your child too thin. On the average, children can handle one or two outside activities. This could mean dance one night and scouts on another. As children get older and more advanced however, participation in dance or sports requires 3 to 5 nights of practice. This is where parents need to make that judgment call for each child. While some children thrive on being busy, others panic at not being able to handle it all. If grades start to seriously slip, then a definite discussion needs to take place as to what needs to be eliminated or at least reduced. Be careful of threatening a child with not being able to attend their next game if homework is not complete. This now creates a problem for the whole team which isn't fair to them. It might be more feasible to miss a particular practice if they fall behind, and let your child get the natural consequence of having to face the coach and team.

In some exceptional situations, you may have a child that will never be a rocket scientist, but is a star in their sport. I know of a very famous hockey player who repeated a grade three times, but was invincible on the ice. Can you imagine if that mother took hockey away from that child? If you do have a child that is a natural athlete, but struggles in a particular subject, then figure out a way to get that child the help they need in that subject so that they can participate in that sport. Please understand I am not talking about the child that doesn't do their homework, but the child who studies and still doesn't grasp the material. We all need to feel competent somewhere in life in order to feel good about ourselves.(Personal power)

Section 7:

IMPROVING RELATIONSHIPS

- A. Attention
- B. Friendships
- C. Getting Revenge
- D. Opportunities
- E. Sibling Rivalry
- F. Stress / Spirituality / Support
- G. Undoing Our Mistakes

ATTENTION

"He's just doing that for attention." How many times have we either uttered or heard those words? How do we really know if they are doing it to get our attention? Check your reaction. Are you irritated, or angry? If you are irritated, chances are, it is for your attention.

Getting our attention can take many forms. As a toddler, it might be wanting you when you are on the phone. As a teenager, it's telling on a sibling. It could be conscious or unconscious. One thing to keep in mind is that regardless of whether a child receives too much attention or not enough attention, both actions will result in attention seeking behavior. How do we know if it's enough or too much? Research has indicated that twenty minutes of one on one time with our child drastically reduces whining and aggressive behavior. It's interesting to hear parents' reactions to that amount of time. Some think, "Is that all?" Others say how will I ever fit that in? Pity the second remark.

Twenty minutes really isn't that much. Ten to fifteen minutes of reading a bedtime story and another five to ten minutes of something else like driving to and from a game, talking about an interest of theirs, or playing a simple game. Remember it needs to be just you and your child. It's too easy to fall into the trap of using this time to nag, criticize, or complain about something that puts you at risk for an argument. We all know how easily an argument can erupt before you even know it's happening.

Another easy trap is giving them attention when they're misbehaving. But what about when they *are* behaving? A simple, "I love it when you two get along" or "you did a nice job" can go a long way. It's so easy to forget to say these things. Don't be too hard on yourself. Maybe this will help. Right now, ask yourself how many times do you let them know you appreciate what they're doing? If the answer is zero or one, think how easy it will be to get better! If you're serious about this, then make yourself a reminder somehow. Sometimes, just writing it down helps. Set a goal. Even saying something once a week is a good start. I'm not talking about empty compliments. Kids recognize those right away. Be specific.

EXERCISE:

List two positive, specific behaviors that you could acknowledge to your child this week that has a pretty good chance of happening.
EXAMPLE: *"I love when you start your homework without me asking you."*

1._____

2._____

FRIENDSHIPS

Friendships can be a tricky matter. They come in all shapes, sizes and personalities. There is always the friend that seems to "use" your child and then dump them for someone else. There is the child that comes over and wants to get out everything and leaves a mess or breaks things. There is also the child that seems to be the "partner in crime." How do you protect kids from these scenes? Quite simply we can't stop every situation. In fact sometimes, the more we want our child to stay away from them, the more they are drawn to them. This is where we say to ourselves, "I might not be able to control their behavior, but I can certainly control mine." So when my child asked if the "messy" kid could come over, I'd suggest that they could go to their house instead. I remember saying "yes" in a weak moment, and sure enough, even though I warned my child to make sure his friend helped with clean-up, he didn't. My child was stuck with having to clean the mess and he did NOT like that.

For the child that seems to cause trouble, you need to consider the stakes involved. It's one thing if they are making prank calls, and totally another if they're going into the woods and experimenting with fire. If the trouble is minimal, then suggest they play together at your house where you can supervise. In this case going to his house wouldn't be allowed. If however they risk run-ins with the law, then that friendship would simply not be allowed. I would hope that the relationship you have with your child is strong enough that they will understand this. If it is not, then that may call for a counseling situation in order to understand what the attraction is to trouble-making friends.

A couple of other suggestions. Keep in mind that three's never work. By this I mean avoid having 3 children play together. One always feels left out. I discovered this both at school and at home. My sons happen to be only 13 months apart, so when one had a friend over, the other one would want to join in of course. That never worked. I was better off letting my daughter have a friend over and letting the boys play with each other. Believe it or not, some of the quietest times in my house were when each child had his or her own friend over. Even though that meant six children, each of mine had their own friend, and it always worked great.

As I already stated in the "emotional intelligence" section, always observe if your child is happy in his relationships with his peers. If they are complaining that they don't have enough friends, and you've noticed that your child is bossy when he's playing with his friends, he needs to gently be made aware of that. The best way to do this, once again, is through self-evaluation. Hopefully through your questioning, they will come to their own conclusion that it's somewhat their own fault.

Occasionally, however they simply do not see it, or don't want to admit it. Unfortunately that is when they come to learn from the school of "hard knocks". They may flit from friend to friend until one day they have no one. It may take this experience for them to finally do some soul searching to realize they are partly at fault. If your child's school has a counselor or a perceptive teacher, you may want to ask school to intervene. At school they could bring in one of his friends who has the initiative and maturity to honestly say what upsets him when they play together. Often hearing it from one of their peers is a real eye-opener.

On another aspect of friendship, when my daughter was old enough to watch her younger brothers we had a "friend" rule that worked quite well. She was allowed to have one friend over, (her friends were quieter). The boys could not, but they were allowed to play at someone else's house, provided I knew the family. Like I said that worked well in our household. You may want to try some version of that when one of your children

Who Says Kids Don't Come With A Manual?

is old enough to watch the others. A caution about letting siblings baby-sit each other. The first time you try it, let it be for a short period of time. Then discuss how it went. I know many families who say they do not trust their children to baby-sit their siblings. Occasional babysitting of sibs is a reasonable expectation. A discussion of ground rules and situations that could arise would be helpful. Expecting a child to baby-sit their sibs full time is a more risky proposition, however. This comes up particularly during summer vacation time. A compromise could be to have the child watch their siblings two or three days a week as a regular paying job. Then the remaining days have a different child care set-up, be it going to day care or having someone else watch your children.

GETTING REVENGE

Getting revenge on parents can be a common reaction in children, particularly when they feel the punishment is too harsh. This fact was confirmed when I was counseling a capable fifth grader as to why he wasn't completing his homework. Without hesitation or remorse he simply stated that he was paying his mom back for grounding him the entire card marking.

Throughout this manual I have discussed discipline, consequences, and other related matters. Continually evaluate the appropriateness of the consequence delegated. Ask yourself if the consequence is reasonable, and related to what they did. Often you can ask them if they think it's reasonable. This is once again part of the positive relationship, negative content message we so often have to deliver to our children. Believe it or not, children are usually pretty honest about level of consequence they are receiving. We also know that some will argue, no matter how small the consequence may be. Sticking with our plans can be difficult. I love parenting expert Jim Fay's response to this; *"I love you too much to argue"*.

Discussing possible consequences BEFORE the offense occurs can reduce needless animosity. Common infractions such as not cleaning their room, coming in past curfew, or incomplete homework can have "preset" consequences, eliminating much arguing. Just remember that consequences need to be natural or logical, relating back to their offense. If you ask them what the consequence should be, and letting them know you will consider it can be effective also. Remember two important steps: 1) You can always delay the consequence if you are not sure about what to do, and discuss it with someone else. 2) If you gave the consequence when you were angry, it is acceptable to ease up on it, explaining to your child, that you said that in anger. As long as you don't do this too often, your

Who Says Kids Don't Come With A Manual?

child will view you as reasonable and human, and won't be apt to want revenge on you.

Louanne Saenz

OPPORTUNITIES

Many parents complain that their children won't open up to them or talk to them. They often ask me to intervene on their behalf. Just like adults however, children have to be in the right mood. Often we ask them to talk when *we* feel like it and not necessarily when they want to. If in fact they do say that they aren't in the mood, you can always respond with, "That's ok, just let me know if you change your mind." Finding the opportunity to talk to them can happen when you least expect it. I find on the few occasions they do take the initiative I really try to drop what I am doing to talk. It is time well spent, and builds the, "Influence bank account" considerably!

Psychologist, William Pollack, author of "*Real Boys*" has devoted most of his practice to boys and their fathers. He suggests ***doing*** something with boys, rather than talking face-to-face. As I've mentioned earlier, his therapy sessions could involve a fishing trip as a way for boys to relax and consequently talk more. I'm not suggesting this be done, but even a trip to McDonalds could do the trick.

Books are another wonderful opportunity to discuss something that is awkward or involves choices. Simply going online and typing in a keyword can result in numerous titles of books and summaries at your disposal. It's much easier to approach a subject if you've just read an animal story, for example where the characters have to make some type of choice. It's often easier to talk about animals and inanimate objects rather than speaking directly about themselves. Sometimes they will then transfer the situation to their own lives, and make a connection that otherwise might never have been made.

Riding in cars are also a great time to discuss things, particularly if you have just one child with you. They can't run away and they know they have an out when they arrive. Be careful not to bring up something too controversial though. I learned that the hard way, and we sat in stone silence for quite a while. It was not pleasant.

EXERCISE:

Think about something you have wanted to discuss with your child.
_____
_____
_____

Now choose one of the techniques above to do it. Plan a specific time to do it.
_____
_____

SIBLING RIVALRY

Sibling rivalry, along with chores and homework would probably rank as the top three concerns of parents. A couple of things you should keep in mind. You can only REDUCE not ELIMINATE sibling rivalry. Secondly rather than focusing on what your children should be doing, I want you to focus on behaviors you can change in yourself.

Let's briefly talk about why sibling rivalry exists. As with any misbehavior the most common reasons are for attention, power or revenge. If they are doing it for attention, you'll most likely know because you will feel irritated with them. What can YOU do? Ignore it. Unless it's a dangerous situation, stay out of it. If it's bugging you either move to another part of the house or ask them to move.

When our children were younger, we were staying at a hotel with an indoor pool and restaurant. The kids wanted to remain swimming and we wanted to grab a bite to eat. We knew they were all strong swimmers, so we let them stay in the pool, while we went to the restaurant next door. What they didn't know was that we checked in on them every five minutes or so. They were getting along great! When we met up with them and I pointed this out, my daughter very matter of factly said, "Oh we only fight when you're around."

Another time our two sons were arguing pretty loudly about something, while I was trying to watch TV. I calmly stated that they had to go argue somewhere else. Their jaws dropped, since they were expecting me to get involved and solve the problem. Never get drawn into those situations. You will find yourself siding with one child over the other. This will create resentment on their part toward both you and their sibling. If it is reaching a dangerous level, then separate them, until they have calmed down enough to rationally discuss a solution. If the situation becomes chronic, then as in any other chronic dilemma, sit

Who Says Kids Don't Come With A Manual?

down with them when everyone is calm. Discuss the problem without taking sides, and listen for options, until they come up with something mutually agreeable. If they can't, then ask if you can make some suggestions. Remember the "rewind the video" trick? This is a good opportunity to use that strategy. The more they practice this process, the better and faster they will become at successfully resolving their disagreements. Don't be interested in who started it. Stick with the facts, giving each one an uninterrupted turn to speak.

The next motivation could be power. You will know this because your reaction is one of anger rather than irritation. Some prevention work may be necessary here. If the situations often center around winning a game, then either don't let them play that for a while or invite other kids to play, not just the two of them. If you notice that one is more often the bully, then talk to that child privately to see what is truly at the bottom of this.

The last motivation could be revenge. Children are usually pretty open about this, stating they are paying them back for one reason or another. Again this may call for talking to that child alone to discuss other ways they could resolve this matter.

Look for patterns. Do they fight more often on weekends when they are together more? How long can they typically play before a major fight does break out? Can you avoid that by having a friend come over or taking one child to another friend's house? Again that ten minute investment of time to drive them could be well worth the effort if it saves 20 minutes of fighting and arguing.

EXERCISE

Think about the last few weeks or so in your home. What have your children fought the most about in your home?

Louanne Saenz

Attention
Power
Revenge

    Based on your answer, determine an appropriate course of action. Revisit this issue every few weeks. If you observe improvement, then by all means acknowledge it. You don't have to go overboard. Just simply state to them that you really appreciate when they can play together without arguing. If you hear one child agree to do something the other one wants, let them know what a considerate gesture that was. It's so easy to ignore when they are doing something right, because we are often so busy pointing out their mistakes.

Who Says Kids Don't Come With A Manual?

STRESS / SPIRITUALITY / SUPPORT

Stress is certainly not in short supply in today's society. Between two working parent households, single parent households, step-families, blended families, divorce, we do not need to go far to find stress. The good news however, is that in studies of resilient children, it was found that just one caring, supportive adult was enough to make a difference.

If we were to designate a stress factor in children's lives, we might begin by assigning a number to stressful events. For example a death or divorce could be a 50, while starting a new grade could be a 5. On the flip side we could also assign numbers to various sources of support in children's lives. Having grandparents or other extended family nearby could be a 20, or being part of a team or club could be a 10. The more support in one's life then would be an obvious way for people to more effectively cope with stress. I emphasize this fact because it often gets overlooked in times of crisis.

People assume that when a very stressful event occurs, their child immediately needs professional counseling. If a strong support network already exists, this may not necessarily be the case. I'm sure we all know of people who seem to survive a tremendous amount of stress, while others can't seem to handle any. While part of this can be due to their personalities, another significant reason is their support system.

One type of support that often gets overlooked is spirituality. I am not advocating any particular type of religion here, but I am suggesting that some type of regular church attendance can be comforting to a child. Remember children love both repetition and tradition and church fits those criteria. I know oftentimes children may complain about going, but giving children this foundation will serve them well for the future.

Every day at school I have lunch with a different grade level. Frequently some type of religious event in a child's life is mentioned, which naturally leads to more discussion of religion. Invariably the students who do attend church or religious instruction regularly enthusiastically chime in, while others will sheepishly admit that they don't attend church. It's not something I ask them. They volunteer the information themselves. What I have asked occasionally is whether they ever pray. I always get the same answer there too. Children are very proud to admit they pray. They haven't yet been tainted with cynicism and doubt. I share this with you because Church is yet another activity that is simple, inexpensive and when approached gently can be a great source of comfort, tradition, and education. Sometimes mothers might be more conscientious about church attendance. If only mom wants to attend, that's always better than no one attending. Besides, when dad sees that he's missing out on a positive experience, it might be incentive enough to join, at least some of the time.

EXERCISE:

List 5 sources of **STRESS** in your child's life, and rank them from most stressful (5) to least (1).

5. _____
4. _____
3. _____
2. _____
1. _____

NOTE: If you have more than 5 SIGNIFICANT sources of stress, this may call for professional counseling.

Who Says Kids Don't Come With A Manual?

Now list 5 sources of **SUPPORT** in your child's life.
5. _____
4. _____
3. _____
2. _____
1. _____

Again be sure that you can list at least five, and if you can't start thinking of how to find more support in your child's life. With email nowadays, kids can keep contact much easier with relatives living far away, as another means of support.

Sometimes, the same source can be BOTH stressful and supportive. School could be an example of this. Perhaps they love the social aspect, but get stressed over grades. List the specifics then where appropriate. The important piece is to decide if it is MORE stressful or supportive.

UNDOING OUR MISTAKES

Second guessing our parenting decisions is inevitable. Some do it more often than others however. I would refer you back to the "Guilt versus Confidence" (section 1A). Parenting more out of guilt than confidence will typically result in second guessing our actions more often. As in any other aspect of our lives, we will make parenting mistakes. Admitting and reducing (never eliminating) our mistakes can go a long way in cementing our relationships with our children. Admitting our mistakes also sets a good example to our kids. The more readily we can acknowledge our mistakes with our children, the easier it will become for them to admit and accept their mistakes. The situations I am mainly referring to are in disciplinary decisions or reactions we might have with our kids when they upset us, because these can both occur rather often.

As was discussed in the section on Reward and Punishment (section 4D), sometimes we may realize the consequence we chose could be a little too harsh. Reducing that consequence and letting the child know you were very angry at the time, shows our human side. Again I warn though, be careful not to do this too often, or your child will quickly learn that you don't mean what you say. This is why it helps to delay the consequence until you have had time to calm down and discuss it with the other parent.

Apologizing for something we said in anger is helpful as well. An effective prevention tactic for these situations is the moment you feel your blood start to boil, warn them to get out of sight, because you are worried you are going to say or do something you will regret.

Who Says Kids Don't Come With A Manual?

Index	Section
Allergies /Antibiotics	5B
Allowances	5A
Attention	7A
Bedtime	5C
Behavior	2A
Chores	5D
Consequences	4B
Discipline	4A
Emotional Intelligence	3B
Empathy	3A
Example	3M
Expectations	3L
Extracurricular Activities	6D
Friendships	7B
Fun	2B
Getting Revenge	7C
Guilt	1A
Homework	6A
Humor	3C
Independence	2C
Influence	4C
Justice	1B
Kitchen Capers	5E
Literacy	6B
Love	2D
Messages	3D
Motivation	4D
No!	3E
Opportunities	7D
Power	2E
Praise vs. Encouragement	3F
Questioning	3G

Quiet	3H
"Reduce not Eliminate",	
"Replace not Erase"	1E
Rehearse	3J
Remorse	3I
Rewards / Punishment	4E
"Rewind the Video"	3K
Sibling Rivalry	7E
Stress / Spirituality / Support	7F
Talking to Your Children	3O
Undoing Our Mistakes	7G
Values	1C
"What Can I Do at Home?	6C
Who Owns the Problem?	1D
You Can Make a Difference	1F
"You Have to Try It.	
You Don't Have to Like It."	3N
Zeroing In on the Issue	1G

REFERENCES

Crary, Elizabeth (1992) *Kids Can Cooperate.* Seattle, Washington: Parenting Press

Crook, William G., (1991*)* *Help for the Hyperactive Child:* Jackson, Tennessee, Professional Books

Fay, Jim (1994) *Discipline with Love and Logic.* Golden, Colorado: Love and Logic Press

Glasser, William (1998) *Choice Theory.* New York: Harper Collins

Goleman, Daniel (1995) *Emotional Intelligence.* Broadway, New York: Bantam Books

Kohn, Alfie (1999) *Punished by Rewards.* New York: Houghton Mifflin

Levy, Raymond, Ph.D, O'Hanlan, Goode, Tyler Nororis (2001) *Try and Make Me*

Mooney, Margaget (1990) *Reading To, With and By, Children*, Richard C. Owen (Publisher)

Pollack, William Ph. D. (1998) *Real Boys.* New York: Random House

Shafer, Jean Ph. D. (1999) *Our Core Democratic Values, Civic Virtues in Action.* Spring Lake Mich., River Road Publishing

Soderman, Anne K., Gregory, Kara M., O'Neill, Louise T. (1999) *Scaffolding Emergent Literacy,* Allyn and Bacon

Printed in the United States
22070LVS00001B/160-201